Steal Away

Poems and Prose

Brenda Cumberlege

Manzanita Writers Press

Steal Away: Poems and Prose
Copyright © 2024 by Brenda Cumberlege

All rights reserved. No part of this book may be used, stored in a retrieval system, reproduced in any manner, electronic, mechanical, photocopy, recording, or using other media without written permission from the author or publisher.

ISBN: 978-1-952314-11-7
Library of Congress Control Number:

    Manzanita Writers Press
    manzanitawp@gmail.com
    manzapress.com

Contact author: cumberlegeb@yahoo.com

All photos and art by Brenda Cumberlege Family Collection
Cover photo by Brenda Cumberlege
Cover and Layout design by Joyce Dedini

Phyllis Louise Blackington and daughter, Brenda.

Dedication

When my mother was alive, I never asked her about her life.
She may have told me personal things. I don't remember.
Now, I wish that I had stories of her life that I could read.
I have written stories about my life so you can know about me.

Brenda Thompson Cumberlege

Phyllis Louise Blackingon at the Great Wall of China.

Contents

Dedication

My Life

Dancing on the Table	14
I Spoke to My Mother	16
Rhymer	17
Swing on a Star	18
Cupid Flew Right By	19
Dancing on Father's Shoes	20
Mr. Perry's Front Porch	21
Odd Jobs Kept Me Going	22
Witch on the Window	24
Snowman in a Bar	25
Move to the Country	27
Dead Man's Pants	29
Lost at Sea	30
Driving Lesson	31

My Four Husbands

Ski Slope to Sailboat	34
Single in the Sixties	36
Uniformed Worker	38
Saved by a Dump Truck in Calaveras County	40
Conversation Overheard	42
Leave the Hose on Jesus Maria Road	44
A Regular Guy	46
Boards Crossing	48
A Blithe Spirit	50
Hidden in the Heart	52
Warm Bodies	54
All the Same	55

Napa Nature Walk

A New Day	58
The Egret at Spreckels' Pier	59
The River Walk	60
Grasshopper	62
Zen Garden	63
The Last Walk	64
Misty Winter Morning	65
Wild Mustard Field	67
Going Deep	68
Floating	69
The Catalpa Leaf	70

Family and Friends

Memories of My Father	74
My Little Sister	75
Sister Stars	76
Silver Ribbon for Tempera	77
For Jim	78
My Older Brother Tom	80
One Bar	81
In the Fair	82
Chasing Cows	83
Marvelous Friend, Norman Prigge	84
Don't Tell Sam	85
I Remember Goldia Schuck	86
Visiting Grace	88
Amy Marries Isabeau	89
Then Came a Raft	90
The Daughter	92
My Son	93
Family Tradition	94
Family Reunion	96
Smitten	97

Surrounded by Nature

Early Stirrings	100
Not Time Yet	101
May Roses	102
Escape	103
August Heat	104
Riding to Hounds	105
Autumn Expectations	106
Christmas Tree	107
Ode to a Poinsettia	108
One More Hour	109

Travel Memories

Escaping the Mundane	112
Old Photograph	113
Mariachis on My Mind	114
Desert Life	115
House on Stilts	116
Mountain Refuge—Ocean Escape	118
Steal Away	119
Life in the Tropics	120
The Pumpkin	122
Wild European Adventure	124
A Dress for Martha	125

History in the Making

Wild Times—Did Anyone Work?	128
Soiree	130
Snake Driving	131
MLK Jr.	132
Land of the Free	133
What Next?	134

Bits and Pieces

The Red Purse	138
Shy Boy	140
The Exit Door	142
A Halloween Tale	144
Post-It Note	146
Suffering	147
Larger than Life	148
Nostalgia	149
Floating Corpse	150
New Old Friend	154

About the Author 156

Brenda's dog Oliver, 2024.

Brenda with grandmother Christina Kron.

My Life

Dancing on the Table

Mostly, when I think of my love for my grandma
I remember her playing music on her upright piano.
She played show tunes, popular songs, and marches
With her fingers flying over the keys.
She played for the "lodge" on Saturday nights,
Whatever the "lodge" meant. I was about four.
Everything about my grandma amazed me.
She was the only one I knew who had a piano.
We didn't have a TV and dancing to the music was
Like being on the stage with Shirley Temple.
Of course, we went to the movies Saturday afternoons.
Grandma's old oak coffee table was our stage.
My father converted an old library table to a coffee table.
His original intention was to make a dining room table.
He didn't plan ahead and one by one the library table legs
Were cut down to even out the table until *voila*,
A sturdy coffee table was the end result.
We loved to visit Grandma's house.
Off would come our shoes and the dancing began.
My brother was about five and we danced as long as she played.
Grandma thought I was her Shirley Temple—the star of the coffee table.
I have been loved by many who thought I was a star,
But the only time I truly thought I was one
Was when dancing with my brother on grandma's coffee table.

Brenda's first photo with her grandmother Christina Kron.

I Spoke to My Mother

I spoke to my mother last night.
A vision of her came into sight—
Though she has been dead for 20 years.
I simply said how I missed her laugh.
She didn't need to reply back.
Just her calming presence laid to rest my fears.
I spoke on as if she was right there
Sitting and listening in her favorite chair.
Then I told her of my present life.
No longer a doting mother, no longer a wife;
How nice it would be to share some family news—
Have a good laugh to chase away the blues.
No voice came back to set my worries free,
Yet somehow, I knew she would never leave me;
Her endless love has power all its own.
I speak to others now to reassure
That my spirit of love for them will ever endure.
I spoke to my mother last night.

Rhymer

Prosetry may work for some,
But I'm just not that one.
I'm a rhymer. That's me.
I love to rhyme my poetry.
My aging life comes alive
As I become the rhyming scribe.
I remember past times
And set them in rhyme.
Stories of joy, some sad
Come to me as I lie awake in my bed.
An imagined life comes into focus
When I set words with purpose.
No two poems are the same.
Rhyming words is like a game.
I have many stories I wish to tell
Even if I don't rhyme them well.
I haven't much of import to say.
Rhyming helps me pass the time away.

Swing on a Star

"Would you like to swing on a star?
Bring moonbeams home in a jar?"
Wonderful words from a song of my youth.
To me, they spoke of an unexplored truth.
There was a great world out there
Floating like stars in the midnight air.
I could pray on a star and somehow know
Of all the places I would someday go.
Picture books with exotic animals,
Storybooks with adventure tales
Of animals in the Arctic wild,
Were my dream escapes as a small child.
I always longed to live a life living free.
All that knowledge created a new me.
Learning new languages to communicate
Expanded my enjoyment with all I met.
I soon explored a world without measure.
I look back now on memories I shall ever treasure.

Cupid Flew Right By

Looking back, I thought I knew about love.
Seems like my aging brain has no advantage.
What a colorful tapestry our romances wove.
So many encounters. So many lost chances.

For every time there are memories that last.
Each season, winter, spring, summer, and fall.
Romantic adventures decorate our past.
Joys and woes; I remember them all.

At ten, hiding alone in the privet hedge,
I watched the paperboy on his bike ride by.
Yet, even then, I thought how it would be
If he dropped his bike and kissed me.

Years have passed and the memories remain.
Much is different. Much remains the same.
I watch as my life slowly passes me by.
Yet a flying cupid still gives me the eye.

Do you think the paperboy ever saw me?

Dancing on Father's Shoes

I remember dancing on Father's shoes.
I held his legs and he held me.
We moved around the room,
One two, one two, one two three.
The beat was steady and we were amazing
Everyone watching us told us so.
Mostly Daddy liked country music.
We must have had it on the radio.
There was no TV. No piano to accompany.
Just records and whatever we could tune in.
I would climb on his shoes and we would begin.
I was small—must have been about four.
I really can't recall anymore.
His big hands on my back, we glided around.
His feet made mine move up and down.
I felt protected and amazingly free.
So short—I barely came to his knees.
We were all very happy in those early days.
I loved my father in so many ways.

Mr. Perry's Front Porch

Our San Mateo neighborhood was like one big family. We kids all went to the same school and our parents were all friends who often played cards together in the evening. We kids were free to go to one another's home and play games or just visit.

On a warm summer's night, parents and children alike could be found sitting on the front steps or a chair placed on the front porch to escape the evening heat as none of us had air-conditioning in those days.

When I was about 10 years old, I had my first music lesson. Mr. Perry and his family lived across the street. He had three children and we were all friends. Mr. Perry loved Enrico Caruso's music. Of course, we didn't have TV in those days and our radios were situated in the living room. But Mr. Perry had a phonograph player that he could turn up and regale the whole neighborhood. The music could be heard way down the street.

I loved the sound of opera. The power of Caruso's voice, the melody and the mystery of the music kept my attention for hours. Mr. Perry invited me to join him on the porch. His wife was busy preparing the evening meal and his three kids were running wild—totally uninterested. I sat quietly on the porch and took in the music that would stay with me all my life.

Mr. Perry never explained the music to me. I didn't know one piece from another. I still don't recognize most operas. Mr. Perry never told me what the music was all about. We just listened to the music.

In my life I have seen many operas. I attended many operas with my father-in-law when I lived in Germany. During my first marriage, I saw Leontyne Price sing *Aida* in Los Angeles. Living in California, the San Francisco Opera house was my favorite location due to its accessibility. Now, I enjoy the productions where we can see "Live at the Met" in the local movie theater.

After all these years, still one of my best memories of classical music is the memory I have of hearing Caruso sing on Mr. Perry's front porch.

Odd Jobs Kept Me Going

I don't remember if we were really poor, but I think we were. The first time I remember that we were different was when I was chosen to help in the lunchroom at school when I was in the fifth grade. Other kids wanted to work there but I was chosen. Probably because I never had lunch money.

Being a kid, I played baseball and field hockey after school and never worried about money. Money was a family matter. Family meant Mom and Dad.

When I was in high school, we moved to the country. At this point in our lives, we were living on money Dad had made years before. My older brother was ever busy with his ham radio and my younger brother and sister just played sports and mostly stayed outside with their friends.

For our move to the country, my dad packed all our belongings into the back of an open truck. On the way to our new home, one of the cushions of our couch blew out onto the road. We never found it. Mom replaced the cushion with a rolled up blanket and that's the way it stayed.

The town was so small that everyone knew everyone. We stood out as the new kids in town. All the locals were involved in farming. The kids were part of a generational tradition. My dad's job had promise but never really panned out. I guess he was drinking a lot at that time but I was too busy to pay much mind. Through thick and thin my mom stood by him. Then, he became disillusioned with life and left my mom and us four kids. There was no anger. No parting good-byes. Dad just left. So mom supported us and we did what we could. I was 14 at the time. My brother, Tom, got a job installing TV antennas. We were both in high school. I did babysitting and even washed the neighbor's car for five dollars.

I never asked my mother where she got her strength to carry on. The old question of heredity and environment lingered in my mind. My grandmother, my mother's mother, was a strong woman who never faltered. She supported herself with a babysitting agency in the Bay Area as long as I can remember until she grew too old. Or, was living in the country our chance to be strong and self-reliant? My home and family were my rock. Times were never easy but we were a strong family even after Dad left.

Our house in the small town had a distinct character all its own. I think it was the only house for rent when we moved to town. It is now hard to believe we lived in the only rental house in the whole town. Looking back, I think it may have been abandoned for years before we occupied it.

Lots of things were peculiar about our house. At one time the whole house had been wallpapered. When we moved in, we had to go room to room stapling the paper back up on the wall. It was just kind of hanging there. None of the windows had curtains or screens which was a problem in the summer.

Mosquitoes were a big problem. Also, privacy. Thank goodness three of the bedrooms were upstairs and mine was one of them.

Downstairs, in addition to my mother and older brother's bedroom, was a large living room and dining room. The kitchen floors had settled and the oven door had to be braced closed with a chair. Otherwise, the house was quite functional although we had no washer and dryer or dishwasher. We managed by hand. The first week in the house, my mom got a local road repair guy to throw some cement into the holes in the cement walk leading to the house. Really the only thing that bothered me a little, was we had no normal light fixtures. Light bulbs hung from the ceiling on long cords.

There was a great old-fashioned movie theater in our town. After living in the town for a few months, some girls and I tried to sneak in. I got caught. The manager asked me what I was thinking. I told him I didn't have the money for admission. So he offered me a job. I was 15. I worked there for the rest of my high school years. I also worked for JC Penny's doing window decorating three days a week. I started that job at age 13. The job started out at Christmas as a gift wrapper. The following year I started changing the window displays. I received 50 cents an hour. My mom worked at JC Penny's at that time and helped me get the job.

Holding down two jobs didn't keep me from getting good grades. But I always had spending money. I never questioned how Mom paid the bills. I guess Dad sent money but I don't know.

Looking back, I realize how blessed I was to live such a carefree life. Several members in the family have had real life challenges. Hopefully, our inheritance is good health. Our environments have changed radically. Those good old days are in the past. Small towns still offer untold opportunities. Although more than fifty years have past, heredity versus environment is still something I puzzle over.

Witch on the Window

A restless child, at twelve I loved to draw—
The new car models, birds, trees, I drew them all.
I entered an art competition not knowing what to expect.
I excelled in my division, so I said, "What the heck."
The prize was to paint a store window in town
On the front of a store, I had never known.
All the paint and supplies would be provided.
On talent alone, the prize would be decided.
I entered a picture of a cauldron, a pumpkin, a cat
And an ugly old witch with a very tall hat.
The window on Chandler's Fabrics was the targeted store
In downtown San Mateo. Who could ask for more.
My picture was chosen for the Halloween theme
Winning first prize completed the dream.
I painted the window and took a short break. Then,
Who should be coming down the street? Mrs. Chandler.
She arrived like a queen in her chauffeured limousine.
She paid no attention to my work of art or to me.
She walked into the store as if she couldn't see.
Well, I was as indignant as I could possibly be;
I had worked all day and was proud of the result.
I wasn't about to accept this blatant insult.
I still had paint, so under the ugly witch I wrote her name.
Now, she could take the walk of shame.
Back at school, the principal was dumbfounded
When to him, my artistic adventure was recounted.

Snowman in a Bar

We lived in a small town in the Valley—
Mom and Dad, my sister, brothers, and me.
The year was nineteen fifty-three.
Dad walked to work, which wasn't very far.
We seldom needed the family car.
My dad was loved by all he knew,
In a small town, there were quite a few.
Walking home from work, he'd stop on the way
At the local bar for a peaceful delay
To the ever-monotonous scene
Of an unfulfilled life of a bucolic routine.
Christmas was coming and my dad had an idea
He offered my services with nary a fear
To paint a snowman and his snow family on the mirror
Behind the long wooden bar, reflecting the life
Of a happy snowman, his kids, and his wife.
I painted the snow family with snowflakes and all.
It was all of winter that I could recall.
It was a rather jolly winter scene
To be painted by a young girl of 13.
I was paid 50 dollars by the owner of the bar.
It was the most money I had ever had by far.
In my life, I've painted pictures of all kinds of things
But nothing compares with that early Christmas scene.

Brenda at age 13 with her first horse, Duchess.

Move to the Country

I think I was born with a love of horses.
I never thought I could own one, of course.
Horses lived in my vivid imagination.
The only horse I ever saw was on Grandpa's ranch.
It pulled a wagon in the apple orchard.
Grandpa gave me an old leather bridle.
I wonder if it had ever been used.
Our neighbor loaned me an old saddle I kept in my room.
Neither of these things ever had any use.
One day Daddy came home from work
And stated we were moving to the country.
He quit his job and had a new one.
We were moving to Colusa in the Valley.
I was thirteen and in the eighth grade.
Daddy proudly declared, "Now, Breni can have a horse."
That was too good to be true, of course.
But it wasn't. Dad meant every word of it.
We moved and my fondest dream came true.
My first horse was a large old one.
It had been a pack horse in the High Sierra.
"Duchess" was gentle and reliable.
Then, our neighbor's son bought a green broke mustang
At the wild horse auction in the Nevada desert.
He didn't have time to train "Smokey" and I obtained a new horse.
Smokey came with his own saddle and bridle.
I guess my parents thought he was a good buy.
Now, I had two horses boarded at the county fairgrounds.
A stable boy fed and watered the horses. I mucked out both stalls.
After school, I ran home—took off my dress and petticoats—
Put on jeans and took the family car to the fairgrounds.
There was no traffic in Colusa in 1953, so no one questioned me.
When I turned sixteen, and took the driving test at the DMV,
The instructor was surprised that I had been driving 4 years.
Smokey was a wild horse. I had to turn the stirrup sideways
And mount him as he strained at the bit and was ready to bolt.
My grandmother was alarmed but my parents didn't seem to mind.
I often wonder what they were thinking.
Maybe my brothers and sister had more urgent cares.
When I was sixteen I worked at a dude ranch.
There were four of us—three guys and a lady my mom knew.

She managed fifteen dude horses at the Feather River Inn
And I rented out horses at the Mohawk Inn in Blairsden.
In the evening we raked mowed hay and collected it on a wagon.
Weekends we had hayrides for the guests at the Feather River Inn.
We had steak Bar-B-Ques, but no one ate the steak
As most of the guests were Jewish and the food was deemed unfit.
So we ate leftover campfire steak every night.
I had a wonderful sixteenth summer.
Twenty years later, again I was living on the San Francisco peninsula.
One Friday, my husband declared, "We are moving to the country!"
To win me over, he added, "So Brenda can have a horse!"
And I did. This time, three horses, so I had horses for my guests in the country.

Brenda and her horses.

Dead Man's Pants

This is a story about my youth.
We were rich in many ways,
But to tell you the truth
We never had much money.
Yet, we always had clothes in fashion;
Dresses, pants, and hats.
Those were the days of Church—
When we all had to look our best.
Mom would buy a fashion magazine
And out came the sewing machine.
Sometimes she sewed all night.
Everything had to fit just right.
From the time I was quite small,
She made dresses and shirts for all.
Both my sister and I and our brothers
Had clothes to compare with the others.
Money was plentiful in our small town
Where prunes and rice were grown.
The other kids went to the city
If they wanted to buy something pretty.
Dad managed a funeral parlor.
Our mom worked full-time, too.
Clothes we had were seldom new.
Mom knew that wool was costly.
Local stores carried cotton, mostly.
So Mom got the idea for free fabric.
Local men who had come to the end of their time
Were laid out in satin caskets quite fine.
You never saw their body from head to toe.
The casket only covered their lower torso.
So Dad brought home their woolen pants.
Mom cut and sewed and made new clothes.
I never worried about what one would see.
The dead man's pants were quite new to me.

Lost at Sea

Not much ever happened in the sleepy valley town.
Its small-town virtue was known all around.
Every house had a front porch where
Evenings were spent enjoying cool night air.
On such a porch, a shy young man and girl met.
It was a prearranged first date set by friends.
And that is where their friendship ends.
He had joined the Navy to see the world.
Yet at 21, "Whitey" had never dated a girl.
Whitey went off to war and was seen no more.
She wrote him a caring letter or two
In the small town there wasn't much else to do.
Returning from high school, the girl came to find,
On the porch, the family Whitey left behind.
Whitey had been washed overboard at sea.
Now she was surrounded by his family.
Father, mother, sister, aunts, they all came to see
The girl who was part of their family history.
"You were his one and only love," they jointly declared.
"We know you would have been his bride."
The girl was polite and tried to not show the amazement she couldn't hide.
The Autumn light faded.
The days passed by.
The girl thought of Whitey and sighed.

Driving Lesson

The autumn harvest was in full swing. The summer crops in the rolling countryside were being gathered from sunrise to sunset. Orchards of prune plums and acres of rice were being harvested in the blazing sun. The hay fields were cut short and the hay bales were being stacked and hauled into the barn for winter fodder. During the growing season the land was filled with crops that grew season after season until winter was on the horizon. Every autumn after harvest the fields sat fallow and the land rested until the next growing season.

All summer the fields were high with alfalfa and oat hay. After harvest, the hay stubble was disked under to enrich the soil. Every summer, after harvest, we were allowed to turn our horses loose in the open fields.

I was 13 years old that first summer in Colusa. My mom was busy and thought I could drive safely, unaccompanied, out into the countryside to water my horse. I don't know why she had so much faith in me. I really didn't know how to drive. Of course, the car had automatic drive. I wouldn't have gotten far with a stick shift! Short of having driven down the driveway to the mailbox and back, I had no driving experience.

I shall never forget driving too fast and practically missing the sharp turn to the field. I swung wide and drove out into the adjoining pasture. Thank God, there was no barbed wire fence—or any fence for that matter—to stop me. No ditch, no obstacle, nothing. I simply made a wide turn off the road and into the field without incident.

Needless to say, that was a driving lesson I shall always remember. I was definitely a dangerous driver at age 13.

Brenda on her honeymoon with her first husband Karl Hiller in Paris, 1958.

My Four Husbands

Ski Slope to Sailboat

My English friend, Annabel, met another Englishman, Fred Noad, when they both arrived from England into the New York harbor. Freddie was an accomplished guitarist on his way to Hollywood and fame and fortune. Annabel was looking for adventure in America. It was 1958.

She made a connection in Squaw Valley, and we became roommates. We worked in the cafeteria morning and evenings and skied all day. I knew the manager and, truth be told, I got all the easy jobs. Evenings we hung out in the beer bar downstairs, mingled with the guests, and danced to the latest tunes on the jukebox. "Play Misty for Me" was the number one tune played in our bar. Partly, because Misty Cumberlege was a popular ski instructor, and very good-looking Englishman teaching with the French ski school. He was my first real crush.

When Easter rolled around, the snow diminished and skiing came to an end. I had no plans for after the season, so I was happy when Annabel asked me to join her on a trip to Corona del Mar. Misty was off to Portillo, Chile for the ski season down under. It was over 60 years before I saw Misty again. I had never been to Southern California so that seemed like an adventure to me. Annabel had a car and we were off.

At first, we stayed at Freddie's apartment. Freddie had many admirers and attended many parties. Annabel accompanied him and made many friends with expats from diverse countries.

One fellow she met was Karl-Heinz Hiller. He was a handsome German, thirty-two, and single. He heard about me and wanted to meet me. He asked if I would like to meet him at the Balboa Yacht Club and crew on his International 14 sailboat. I had never been on a sailboat before. (The International 14 was the smallest of the ocean racing class.) We amazed everyone when we won the Easter Regatta and won the silver cup. We were married two months later. We were very much in love and had two wonderful children.

Karl-Heinz Hiller

Small boat racing in the Mediterranean, year unknown.

Single in the Sixties

Living in Germany from 1962 until 1968, I enjoyed my life as a single woman. I had my children but with family support during a separation from my husband, Karl, I was free to enjoy life in Heidelberg.

"Sex, Drugs, and Rock and Roll" was the anthem of the sixties. Well, I was never part of the drug scene—not even marijuana. Germany was free of drugs as far as I was aware. But Rock and Roll was the rage. Everywhere Nancy Sinatra was heard singing, "These Boots were Made for Walking." "Hello Dolly" was also popular in Germany. And everyone loved the Beatles.

Germans loved everything American. I hung out with an international group of people. There were several Hungarians, Swiss, and Egyptians as well as Americans. The popular after-hour night clubs were owned by Egyptians. The *Key Club* was only accessed by a password given through a small window in the entrance door. *Atif's* was the other Egyptian-owned bar. Some Heidelberg students frequented the clubs but they were mostly visited by an older crowd. Both bars had grand pianos and music was played late into the early morning. Cool jazz was in fashion. My sister and a daughter of one of my mom's friends also came to live with me during this time.

I remember having my clothes made by a seamstress in a fashionable salon. I wore knee-high white leather boots. (I was a lot slimmer then.) I guess I could say my sixties were my best years. I was in my mid-20s.

In the summer, I spent time with the children in Palamos, Spain. Karl had purchased a lot in a new subdivision overlooking the Mediterranean. My sister and I helped furnish the house shortly after it was built. She was only with me one summer. Then she returned home to finish college in Berkeley. Karl and I never spent time together in Spain. It was his house but I had the freedom to go there with my friends. Marianna Jost, my Hungarian girlfriend, and I would drive my little Volkswagen from Heidelberg to Palamos in one day. I had my two kids. She had a son. She spoke Hungarian with her son. I spoke English with my kids. We spoke German together. While in Spain we both spoke Spanish in town. Days were spent swimming and eating ice cream.

I would have been happy living in either Germany or Spain. I was happy being single. I could live easily with my child support. Things were very inexpensive in Europe in the sixties. But the children were growing up and it was time for them to start school. Karl suggested we make an attempt at reconciliation. He accepted a prestigious job in New Jersey. We moved back to America and gave it a try. I felt very alone in New Jersey. After two years, we agreed the best thing was to finalize our divorce. The children and I moved to Belmont, California. Karl moved to New York.

Author Brenda Cumberlege, Heidelberg, Germany, 1966.

Uniformed Worker

The new shopping center was in a lovely tree shrouded area and the center of the community. Retail shops, a new restaurant, real estate office, and some professional offices were already occupied. A new bakery was the last of the spaces to be filled.

I was working at I. Magnins at the time selling cosmetics. It was a good job, if not rather monotonous, and it paid well. I realized in a short amount of time that my daily employment meant that I would be dealing with women almost exclusively. I also sold perfumes which brought a very few men into the store. I felt trapped in a world of women.

The shopping center was close to our home. I was divorced and living with my two children less than a mile away. From our home, the children could walk to school and walk to the shopping center.

I reasoned that a job in the shopping center would be more convenient for me and the children. Also, I reasoned that I was not likely to meet a husband and prospective stepfather for my children selling cosmetics at I. Magnins in Palo Alto.

That is when I got the idea to apply for a job at the new bakery in the shopping center. There had been a sign in the window of the newly completed bakery advertising the need for bakery help. I had never worked in a bakery.

Although many women had applied for the job, there was a problem. The bakery was a union shop. I had no idea what that was; but I later learned it meant you had to have a union card in order to work there. I applied for the job and was told I needed a union card. The shopping center owner was a likable Italian who needed to staff the bakery and he asked if I had ever worked in one. Instead of answering "no," I told him that I had a relative in Germany who had a bakery. (Actually, it was a friend's father that owned a bakery in Germany). "Good enough," he replied. Then he said, "Come on," and we drove to South San Francisco to the union hall. Within hours, I had a union card.

I enjoyed working in the bakery. The union card indicated I was an experienced bakery worker. That meant I knew how to slice bread with a bread machine—an easy skill. The only objection to the job came from my mother who was horrified that I had to wear a white uniform. I think she really liked me selling cosmetics. It was a more glamorous occupation.

The job in the shopping center didn't last long. A young man, Barry Young, came in one morning for a cup of coffee. He had just finished filing for divorce with the attorney also situated in the shopping center. He and a friend had just bought an art gallery and were looking for a manager. He asked me if I knew anything about art. I told him, truthfully, that I had visited the major art museums in Europe. I was hired. That began a long and adventuresome relationship and I married Barry Young in 1969.

Brenda and second husband Barry Young.

Saved by a Dump Truck in Calaveras County

At the time, in 1976, we really did think we could earn a living raising worms. Seems far fetched now, but at the time we were looking for any new sort of employment. My husband Barry had been a Fuller Brush man in the San Francisco Bay Area. Needless to say, that was no longer to be his occupation. It was 1976 and the total population of the county was less than 16,000. Most of those people were only part-time residents. I was a realtor at the time. Living out in the country, we were miles from any housing development. Our home in Mountain Ranch was our dream home but it was in a very remote area. Living in the country presented a challenge.

Worm farming was touted in newspapers and magazines as a new way to make a living in the country. It appeared to be organic and a good way to dispose of waste. Some proponents of the business were even suggesting the worms were a good source of protein and could be eaten. Worm recipes actually were found in some San Francisco papers.

Worm farming captivated people of all social status. You could have a small recycle bin in your basement where the worms could have an even temperature and eat your organic garbage. Small areas set aside for worm farming were used to dispose of old vegetables, fruit peelings, and coffee grounds just to name some of the organic waste fed to the worms.

Or, as was the case in Mountain Ranch, you could build a large wooden trough on acres of land. Overhead sprinklers were installed to keep the soil damp. Night lamps shone over the worms to keep them warm in the evenings. As long as they were fed regularly, they didn't disappear into the ground beneath the bins.

We were told the local nurseries and garden centers were eager to buy the "worm castings" as they were fashionably called. Keeping the worms sorted from the castings only required a sorting frame made of fine mesh wire.

A mutual friend knew the market and encouraged us to make a decision to invest $7,000 in a starter farm on our ten-acre ranch. We were introduced to a local man who encouraged us and others to invest. We felt we were in good company. The gentleman was a retired military man who spoke convincingly of the business opportunity of raising worms. He wanted to sell us part of his worm farm so we went to visit him to discuss the business of worm farming.

While we were there, an old derelict dump truck came bumping down the dirt road. "Looks like you have a visitor," my husband said half-jokingly.

"Nope," answered the worm farmer. "That is my weekly supply of chicken manure to feed the worms."

"How much does a dump truck filled with chicken manure cost?" we asked innocently.

"About $500," came his answer.

Doing some quick calculations, we realized the only winners in this operation were to be the gentleman farmer and the worms.

Thankfully, the dump truck arrived when it did. We remember with smiles our close call as farmers—glad for the adventure and glad we held on to our $7,000.

Conversation Overheard

In a small town like San Andreas, everyone knows everyone else's business. It may be the county seat, location of the government center, and one would expect some privacy; nevertheless, word gets around about events of the prior twenty-four hours pretty fast. Local gossip is more informative than the local radio station. The post office is the daily meeting place for most of the locals, as that is where mail gets picked up and there is always time to hang around and read the postings on the ever-changing bulletin board.

Once in a while, a newcomer comes to town. They are easy to spot in this small community—particularly in the post office. Two such persons were engaged in conversation one early morning when I stopped by to grab my mail and check the bulletin board. They were two ladies clearly from out of the area. They must have stopped to post their mail. They were dressed in business attire. One had on a dress and stockings and smelled of expensive perfume. The other had on a smart-looking suit. I was curious as to what their business was in our small town. I was in no hurry, so I paused to eavesdrop.

"Helen! Haven't seen you in a long time!" one lady exclaimed to the other.

"I've taken on a new career, Joan," she answered.

I became interested on the spot. I had been a real estate broker for over twenty years and knew it was time to look for other opportunities. Maybe, this was the break I was looking for. Times had changed. The buyers from the Bay Area had recently curbed their desire to settle in the foothills. People were becoming more cautious about land and country investments due to the economy. This was directly affecting my income. So I listened.

"What kind of career could you possibly have undertaken in the short time since I saw you last?" the one named Joan asked.

Helen had apparently known Joan for some time in the past. So she unabashedly related her change of profession when queried.

"I've given up real estate sales and become a real estate appraiser," came Helen's answer. "Of course, I had to meet some requirements. I took two appraising classes at Sacramento State and worked under an appraiser for a short while. But I did it in less than two years. Because I have my Real Estate Broker's license, some of the requirements were waived."

"Didn't you have a state exam?" asked Joan in amazement.

"Sure, but it wasn't much different from the Broker's exam," replied Helen with a smile.

I kind of lost the thread of their conversation after that. That was the solution I was looking for. A change in career! I went home and explained to my husband how I wanted to become an appraiser. I had no doubt that the overheard conversation was directed to my ears as the chance I was looking for. I closed my real estate office and within two years I was appraising property in Calaveras County. Though I never saw those two women again, I credit my success in business to that overheard conversation. Were they angels?

Leave the Hose on Jesus Maria Road

I like to think back on driving that long road home—
Eight miles from Mokelumne Hill. Always alone.
Our newly-built farmhouse sat high on a hill.
The narrow road snaked upward; I remember it still.

Rain or shine, I drove slowly home at night
Always glad for the afternoon setting sunlight.
My job as a realtor kept me busy all day.
Enjoying nature's beauty was better than the pay.

While driving home, there was always a new surprise.
Suddenly something new would catch my eyes.
Animals of all types crossed the paved road—
Deer, snakes, rabbits, an occasional toad.

I even saw a mountain lion in the years I drove home.
He had a track from which he seldom would roam.
But the strangest by far, was the sight of the wolf spider—
Also known by the common name Tarantula.

They move slowly, drifting, like puppets on a string
As they cross the warm pavement in the early evening.
I stopped my car to observe the amazing sight.
There must have been a hundred that early autumn night.

Their hairy bodies are so amazing to see.
I'd seen them many times before—they don't frighten me.
Parked on the edge of the deserted country road,
I noticed something quite out of place.

As I watched the spiders crossing the road, I saw
A long new garden hose going over the bank.
Someone was supplying water from a water tank.
I followed the trail of the hose down the hill.
It ended in a large pot grove hidden from the road.
Locals didn't grow marijuana plants at all.

Who could be watering a garden outside of the law?
When I got home I called the police.
Illegal pot farms on my hill were not to be.
I was very concerned about illegal activities.

Before I was aware, my husband fetched all the hoses.
He said we could use them to water the roses.
"Quick, take them back!" I shouted in alarm.
"The police are coming to visit our home!

We don't want them to think the hoses are ours!
They will surely think that if they are in our yard!"
They were taken back to the scene of the crime.
No more illegal pot farms were discovered in our time.

A Regular Guy

In my youth, I was a romantic dreamer.
My life was filled with movies and escape.
We lived an ordinary life in the fifties.
But I knew there was a big world out there.
Faraway lands and places for me to discover.
Glamour and travel were calling to me.
Upon reaching fifty, I saw life differently.
I was ready to live alone and settle down.
Being successful in my career, life changed.
I was able to purchase a house on my own.
For the very first time, I lived alone.
I could be independent—the children all grown.
I was resigned to a quiet life in San Andreas.
Having tasted so much of the world,
My little house and garden were all I craved.
Very unexpectedly, a local man asked me to
Join him in a golf tournament in Nevada.
I knew Bob from business in the area.
We had never met socially.
When he first asked me out to lunch
I thought it could be for business.
Then he asked me to join him in a golf tournament.
I was concerned about what others might say.
My mom said, "Brenda, no one cares about what you do!"
So I joined him and fell in love.
We were happily married for almost 25 years.

Brenda with her third husband Bob Eastman.

Boards Crossing

Some of my happiest memories are with my family
Camping at our special spot by the Stanislaus River.
We fished and swam, and floated in the lazy river.
Bob and I had many memorable moments there.
As time wore on, the old access road was a challenge.
Bump Bump Bump. The old truck bumped down the road.
The rutted logging road made traveling slow.
The dust cloud rose around the battered old truck.
Springtime, the loggers would again drag the cattle guard
Over the ground and attempt to make it level once more.
The pain, from bouncing down the dusty road,
Would soon be replaced by the joy of seeing the river.
Much work was needed to establish the campsite.
Bob and his son knew the routine and got the work done.
Cooling evenings and fading light signaled time for the campfire.
Once again, the bats would feed on the darting insects.
Fragrant crackling pine-pitch scented the fresh air.
All old memories were re-lived, joined by quiet moments,
As the growing campfire warmed the aching bones.
A dimming light blanketed the glowing campfire.
Long lost summer dreams sparked once again
In the smoldering coals of the dwindling light.
Nothing can replace the peace we felt those summers
Our families gathered together by the river.

Bob Eastman

Floral painting by the author.

A Blithe Spirit

What is a "blithe spirit"? The New World Dictionary defines a blithe spirit as, "showing a gay, cheerful disposition; carefree." The word comes from a root word meaning to shine.

Misty was a blithe spirit and so much more. Yet his wife Brenda shall always think of him as childlike and kind. He never had a critical word to say about anyone. And, he didn't tolerate gossip or words that belittled anyone. He was gentle spoken and one would listen when he spoke. His cheerful disposition made him many friends.

Misty was a British citizen and was proud of his English heritage. And yet, unlike many, he never criticized America. He loved America and the American people. He was happy living in Angels Camp and even adjusted well to assisted living at Foothill Village in Angels Camp. The staff loved him and he felt like he was at home there. Brenda could no longer meet all his needs and was forever grateful for all the love and care the senior care facility provided.

Misty had lived all over the world. Born in St. Tropez, France, Misty was the oldest of four children from his father's second marriage. He had an older brother and sister from his father's first marriage. Tarik, born three years after Misty, moved to California in the fifties. Tarik was a vegetable broker and offered Misty a job. Misty joined him in Stockton. Misty wasn't cut out for the vegetable business. So he made friends and moved to Squaw Valley as a ski instructor.

Tarik died many years before Brenda had a chance to meet him. Misty is survived by Tarika Brink, a favorite niece of Misty. His sister, Claudine, lives in Mallorca, Spain. His youngest brother lives at the Sea Club in Mallorca. The Sea Club was once Misty's home that later became a resort hotel run by the family. Misty spent many years there in his youth enjoying the people and swimming and sailing in the Mediterranean.

He returned to Spain after many years of travel; married, settled down and became a father to his only child, Henry. Misty loved his little farm in Andalusia. He spoke of it many times. He loved working with the soil. He had fruit trees and some animals. Misty loved dogs. His wife was an avid horsewoman. His son now lives in Bangkok, Thailand. He and his son were very close. They traveled together and enjoyed swimming and skiing.

Misty loved family, skiing, sailing, travel, fast sports cars, BMW motorcycles, playing golf, watches, and women. He could recite poetry and had a great singing voice. The pastor at the Congregational Church wanted him to join the choir. The whole world loved Misty. He married three times. He lived in many places and had many friends.

Brenda met Misty skiing at Squaw Valley in 1958. They both worked at the Bear Valley Lodge in the evenings and skied all day. Misty was a ski instructor.

Misty was Brenda's first love. But the time wasn't right and after ski season they went their own separate ways. Fifty-five years passed. They had not seen one another in all that time. Misty's son, Henry, had just put Facebook on Misty's iPhone. Brenda was a widow and thought how lucky men were that they could be found on Facebook—unlike women who change their last names when they marry. People like "Cumberlege" could be looked up and found on the internet—and he was. They married on Valentine's Day, 2014. So that's what happened and the rest is history. Misty passed away October 3, 2019.

Mistal "Misty" Cumberlege

Hidden in the Heart

My first love was my last love. Passion never dies.
The heart holds many secrets. Real love never lies.
It sat dormant in the heart just ready to surprise.
58 years and three marriages separated me
From a forgotten love awaiting to be set free.
He was my tender first love when I was eighteen.
He was a 22-year-old ski instructor—tall and lean—
I was the downhill racer that captured the scene.
We had no money and our future was vague.
We went our own way for over five decades.
I was happily married to husband number three
Then without warning he died rather suddenly.
I reminisced over the past and passions I had known.
I really didn't want to spend my life all alone.
A search on the computer showed me the way
 And I found that lost love the very same day.
We married after two months of unexpected joy.
Although time had passed, to me he was the same boy.
It was a passion of the heart once again set free
A very special hidden love known only to me.

Brenda and Misty in Italy 2016.

Warm Bodies

The dog races down the long-deserted hall.
There are no morning sounds to greet us.
The long night exits with the rising sun.
I pass the closed doors and somehow know
Your door will be open and you will be waiting.
The dog jumps up onto your bed;
I climb slowly up to caress your waiting body.
How long have you been lying there awake?
Do you really know it is I that is next to you?
Slowly, we greet one another with our hands
And lips and know there is yet one more day.
Your lips are dry. I moisturize them.
Thankfully you sit up and wish to rise.
I get the wheelchair and take you to the toilet.
You still enjoy me dressing you for breakfast.
We are the first to arrive in the dining room.
The night shift has put out your cornflakes and milk.
Warm water replaces coffee but the fast is broken.
We don't talk. Sometimes I sing or recite poetry.
Later, I take you to the TV room where I watch the news.
You are in your own private world. The dog joins you.
Once more to the toilet; then the morning breakfast.
You enjoy what they serve even if you don't eat it all.
Then you are ready for a morning nap. We kiss.
I leave and return to a world without you.

All the Same

"Now, you have married for the fourth time," she stated.
"Tell me, how do you respond to four different men?"
The astonished responder did reply, "They are all the same."
"I imagined so," answered the inquisitor.
Feeling some explanation needed, the responder went on—
"We are all trying to get by in this world. We all seek love.
We are young with the challenges of youth.
We get older with all new experiences and demands.
You have been married over 50 years to one man.
I have been married over 50 years to 4 men.
Mom used to say, 'They all put their boots on one foot at a time!'
I think I now know what she meant. I'm 80 now
And I remember them well. My life hasn't changed.
I loved them all but as I recall they were all the same."

Sculpture by Brenda's friend, Miles Metzger.

Napa Nature Walk

A New Day

As I slowly approach him on my morning walk,
The small dark lizard scurries under a flat rock.
Pale pink mares' tails streak the sky
Adding color to the awakening countryside.
Blossoming trees add their white flowers.
Silhouetted against a pale blue sky,
New buds pulse forth upon gently swaying branches.
The meadows, still shrouded in an early mist
Infuses the bucolic scenery in a mystical peace.
A flock of Canadian geese call out a greeting
As they head north after the long winter.
My heart stirs with expectation as the wonders
Of Nature remind me of the passing of seasons.
A fellow walker, also glad to be enjoying the fresh air,
Nods a greeting with a welcoming smile.

The Egret at Spreckels' Pier

He's always there, the egret at Spreckels' pier.
He parades along the rocky river bank.
In reality, the pier is no longer there,
And long ago the Spreckels moved away,
But the lone egret still stands his ground.
On the wooded knoll above the river,
The redwood trees stand testament
To stories of long-ago riches gained from sugar.
A hard-packed path, from the property
Once known as the Spreckels' estate,
Still leads down to the area where once
A boat landing stood on the Napa River.
Horse-drawn carriages ferried passengers
Coming from and going to San Francisco.
But now, only local fishermen use the area
Where once the busy pier stood.
The egret waits upon some fisherman's
Bits of fish to reward his patience.
Sometimes, he sits in the trees expectantly, and
Sometimes, this majestic creature strolls past me
Confidently, as if to say, "I am part of this history."

The River Walk

I didn't even know the Napa River was blocks from my new home. I moved into The Meadows independent living apartment the same week as the Coronavirus shelter-in-place came into effect. The only way my family knows where I am is to spy my balcony through the redwood trees from the front parking lot by the entrance to the facility.

Moving in happened so fast that I didn't have time to process all that was going on. It was March 2020—the Ides of March. Not only a turning point in Roman history but also my own. I knew about the virus but didn't even own a mask yet. Even more awkward was the fact my TV wasn't hooked up as the Xfinity people were reluctant to enter and sign a release stating they were virus-free. I didn't really know what was going on.

Yet here I was—really glad to be settled as I wanted to be closer to family and begin my life as a recent widow. I began my exploring of the grounds at The Meadows with my dog, Molly. My first surprise was all the mallard ducks that frequent the grounds in winter. They waddle around quite tame, and looking up, I was happy to see hot air balloons drifting by. Later flights of geese would grace the sky. Resident crows welcomed me with their cawing.

While moving in, I was surprised to see a development across the street called River Yacht Club. I didn't even know the river was in the area. Molly and I set off to see the river. Unfortunately, the subdivision has a locked gate. I walked a little farther and was delighted to see an amazing dirt path to the river. The branches of large trees reach across the path casting shadows of tranquility. In the summer these trees cast shade and make the walk pleasant year-round.

In March, I was greeted at the river by a Great Heron, an egret, and a flock of blackbirds. A little later in the season, I spied a river otter and later other otters and then just as mysteriously they were gone. Ducks and geese come to the river to nest. Soon there was a mother duck with her brood and later a mother goose with her goslings. My walks to the river always hold surprises. Although there have always been fishermen at the river, I have yet to see a decently sized fish. Mostly the men, and sometimes families, just come to the river as I do for the surprises it holds. Colorful kayaks decorate the river almost daily.

The round trip walk to the river is a little over two and a half miles from the front of The Meadows. Now, it is autumn. I look forward to the return of the birds and cooler days. I carry water with me for both myself and the dog. You can drive down an adjacent street and check it out. You won't be disappointed.

Black heron photo by author.

Grasshopper

My eyes are fixed upon a glorious brown grasshopper.
He is sitting contentedly on a smooth round rock.
He glances my way. If only we could talk.
I'm not sure if he sees me. He has a look of disdain.
Does he know how I am exercising a bit of restraint?
My search for such as he, has led me here.
Now, confronted by his look I instantly fear
If I capture him, it will be sorrow I feel.

I am told grasshoppers make wonderful fishing bait.
'Til now worms on a hook have been my fish's fate.
My Mason jar sits empty awaiting the capture.
The joy I feel gazing on the still brown creature
Makes me forget the large trout deep in the pond.
He sits peacefully sunning himself without a care.
Do I really want to hook this grasshopper unaware?
Or should I just be patient and happy to see
A glorious brown grasshopper looking back at me?

Zen Garden

I sit cross-legged on my lawn overlooking the town
I breathe deeply as I watch the evening sun go down.
An elusive butterfly winks at me and glides past.
I wish with my heart for this moment to ever last.
The yard still warm from the quiet sunny day
Offers up a respite I can find no other way.

A small brown lizard winks at me and pauses on a rock
Just long enough for me to welcome him in silent talk.
My eyes smile at my joy from sharing this special time.
All is in harmony evincing a peaceful clime.
Fluffy evening clouds disburse and float away—
I welcome the evening quiet completing this special day.

I stretch back and lie down on the still warm ground.
I marvel at the beauty welcoming me all 'round.
Crushed blades of fresh green grass intoxicate me
All of the surrounding nature sets my spirit free.
A dark bird soars high in the golden evening sky
I rejoice that nature has given me another perfect day.

The Last Walk

Shadows of the dancing leaves make patterns on the sun-dried earth.
Dried leaves crunch under foot awaiting the evasive rains.
Six Canadian geese fly south in anticipation of winter.
All is faded and gray. Brown earth has an exhausted look paled by the sun.
The hard-packed earth reminds one of the years of compression
Caused by horse drawn carriages and pounding feet.
Occasionally, a breeze cools my warming body.
My jacket, now tied around my waist, creates a warm unwanted weight.
A little red tongue hangs out of my thirsty panting dog.
Rain is needed to clean the air and nourish the earth.
My joints still respond to the long walk in the afternoon heat.
Oh, how I wish for the smell of wet leaves and cooling air.
Morning fog and billowing clouds decorated the early autumn sky.
Now, the earth sits still awaiting the evening light.
A yellow butterfly flutters and darts in a drying yarrow plant.
The mellow afternoon light is gently fading.
A harvest moon will soon bring a new promise of life's renewal.
Seasons change and remain the same.
Dancing shadows, Canadian geese, a yellow butterfly, all new
Surprises that keep my mind entertained with life's beauty.

Misty Winter Morning

A misty drizzle drifts silently down through the morning fog.
The slate-gray asphalt reflects the early lights from the restaurant.
The receding tide of the lazy brown river drifts slowly past.
The black wrought iron railing is all that separates me from the
Dark muddy banks of the exposed river shore.
A blue heron stands majestically surveying the peaceful scene.
Too early to meet my companions, I gaze aimlessly ahead.
Small birds fly effortlessly across the foggy surroundings.
Occasionally a patch of blue sky appears promising a fairer day.
My yellow umbrella shields me from the foggy drizzle.
I tell myself I should come this way more often.
Aroused from my reverie, I hear my companions.
Reluctantly, I whisper a silent goodbye and depart the lazy river.

Painting by author. Acrylic on canvas board.

Wild Mustard Field

I am enveloped in a golden mustard field.
I am folded into its amazing beauty.
A poem writes itself onto my heart.
There are no words to describe the moment.
I am humbled by nature's endless bounty.
Bees buzzing. Endless sunshine.
Rows of grapevines shining in the sun.
Color vibrates like a crafted sonata.
I listen to nature's rhythmic sound of yellow.
My body is filled with all that surrounds me.
I have seen miles of wild mustard.
The fields are a backdrop for the oncoming season.
Now standing in the midst of this wild explosion,
I celebrate the encompassing moment of grandeur.
As the buds break forth on the grapevines,
The work of the annual mustard field comes to an end.
The plant is enfolded into the earth to enrich the soil.
Hopefully, the nematode threat has been erased.
Once again, it's time to anticipate new life in the vineyard.
I shall hold these golden memories close to my heart.

Going Deep

The Napa River was high. The gentle rain came down.
No fishermen arrived due to the stormy water.
The wind was gusty. The fish went low.
Anxious people stayed home.

No dogs, no children, no walkers to be seen.
A raincoat for protection, my mind took a stroll
Along the beaten path my dog knows so well.
The Coronavirus isolates us all.

The weather offered a chance to escape.
Cool air and fading afternoon light;
Winter days we know won't last—
Like fish we go deep and wait for the storm to pass.

Floating

In the cool air and fading afternoon light,
I take a river walk to welcome the night.
The long rainy days are no comfort to me.
I mull over today and what is yet to be.
Winter days we know won't last. My thoughts
Like fish go deep and I wait for the storm to pass.

The tide carries flotsam and jetsam silently by.
Nothing of importance catches my eye.
The storm has caused this mass to move
Above silent waters as the rain falls above.
Below the surface, my thoughts tumble on
Unmoved by the tide and the floating jetsam.

Oh, that my troubled thoughts would flee
And float in the ebb tide out to the sea.
Not even fishermen arrive due to the storm.
Alone, I move briskly just to keep myself warm.
As I walk along the path, I discover new energy.
I cast out my troubles and let them float free.

The Catalpa Leaf

The golden Catalpa tree shed its precious leaves
Late that autumn after a violent storm.
The fan-shaped leaves had bejeweled the lone
Tree for longer than usual that year.
Now, the leaves lay rain-soaked on the wet pavement.
Golden leaves, that glistened no more, lay awaiting
The final stage of their glorious worldly life.
Like the Catalpa leaves, the girl's life will be enjoyed
For all the beauty it shares with the world.
Her shining life will burst forth in golden flying sparks.
Then, as the dwindling light of summer wears on,
Her life will mature into the golden essence
Of all that unique character she alone reflects.

The precious untarnished life of the golden leaves
Were challenged only by the violent winter storm.
So, too, the girl must weather the raging storms.
Just as new leaves will again appear on the trees in spring,
Again, nature will amaze us with the shape unique only to them.
The girl will change and grow. A new color will emerge.
Slowly the green will mature into gold and the leaves will fall.
A new glorious season of nature's beauty will be celebrated.

Brenda enjoying nature.

Brenda's family photos.

Family and Friends

Memories of My Father

Large loopy letters amble across a well-worn page.
It is the best memory I have of my father.
I remember his stature. I remember his face.
But mostly, I remember his handwriting.
There was a wonderful freedom in it.
I don't have many other memories of my father.
Still, his handwriting remains a sign of his carefree spirit.
It reflects the joy for the life he wanted to live.
It was alcohol that ended his life so soon.
However, the inner man he showed his family
Was present in the heartfelt love he freely gave.
In the pages of the old, much-used telephone book
I peruse the personal and business addresses he penned.
I don't have a letter or note to treasure
Telling of the deep love he felt for me.
Only the old address book and his handwriting
Reminding me of a gentle spirit
Long ago departed, yet ever present in my mind.

Brenda's father Thomas Aubrey Thompson and her son Christopher Hiller.

My Little Sister

To have a little sister is a joy.
Thank God Mom didn't bring home another boy.
We shared everything as we grew.
Even though our ages limited what we knew.
Mom and Dad loved their little one;
While Tom and I were out having fun.
I just remember her blonde, curly hair.
Oh little sister, I wasn't quite aware.
Little did I know of her loves and fears
As we stumbled along through the years.
Daddy smoked a pipe and we sat on his knees
As he read to us the Sunday funnies.
Little Robert, our adventuresome cousin, came
He added laughter to all our games.
Verlyn, my sister's best friend came along—
Then I graduated high school and I was gone.
Girl Scouts and skiing were all part of the plan
Until my little sister discovered men.
Off to distant Germany at an early age
All of a sudden, the world was our stage.
Then back to life in Laguna Beach with no money.
She lived a married life as a hippie. All was sunny.
She raised two daughters and worked to stay alive.
Looking back, I'm surprised we both survived.
Many romances have come and gone—
Now, together we remember and sing the widow's song.

Sister Stars

You can be Ginger Rogers or Betty Grable,
They like to sing and dance.
I'll be Barbara Stanwyck or Lauren Bacall
Since they were the toughest babes of all.
And we can film our movie in France.
I just want to make a movie
Where we both can shine.
We'll rehearse until we know every line.
Forgetting all the world around,
We'll rehearse, sunup till sundown.
We will make up nefarious deeds
And we will choose our own male leads.
Someone from the past will do—
Bogart for me and Jimmy Stewart for you;
Close-ups made especially for two.
I don't know the plot this early on,
But you will sing a marvelous song.
I'll probably kill someone who deserves to die.
Might have to do it in the next reel—
Want relief and happiness for all to feel.
Later, we'll gather at the Carmel coffee shop
When they see us, all chatter will stop.
They will smile and they will stare
Really pleased that we are there.
We will be Sister Stars known everywhere.

Silver Ribbon for Tempera

I breathe out a silver ribbon of love.
It floats over mountain tops of pain
And caresses deserts of anguish.
It reaches out to comfort you.
No rain or hail can dampen its path.

The silver ribbon encompasses you.
It is there for you to hold.
The silver ribbon wraps around you.
You can feel its warmth.
The ribbon of love enters your heart.

Although we are apart, we are not alone.
Love knows no boundaries.
I breathe out gently so as not to startle you.
Breathe in slowly to inhale the love.
See the silver ribbon I have sent you.

For Jim

A cowboy hat and a little toy gun
You roamed the yard in San Mateo
In your imaginary land
Blessed by the California sun.
How grand it was that the neighbors had
A ranch somewhere for you to join
As they vacationed there in the summertime.
I knew you longed for our own retreat.
Sadly, that was beyond our family means.
You were content in your cowboy shirt
And rugged cowboy jeans.
Then you grew up and became a man
But still held on to the imaginary land.

You were so happy when you found your country home
Where you and Joanne could finally roam
Discovering all the sweet surprises
The land and old ranch house held in store
You need not just imagine anymore.
Years went by and the ranch was a place
Where one and all could find their space.
When Bob died, I followed you there—
We could play Scrabble with nary a care;
Peace was always in the air.

Then the fire came with a fury
Man and terrified animal had to scurry
To avoid Nature's wrath all around—
And then your dreams burned to the ground.
In my mind, I'll always see
That peaceful ranch, the barn, the trees.
Your imaginary ranch is no more.

Now, the real ranch is gone.
It was so perfect all along
Until that fateful day.
So much of life is in our minds.
Memories of long-ago times.
I take heart to know there was a boy long ago
Who dreamed big and the dream did grow.
The imaginary ranch became real.
Life is filled with precious memories.
Many of mine are with you.

My Older Brother Tom

My youth was spent doing my best to keep up with my brother Tom.
We ran the streets and climbed the trees and were seldom home.
The summer cherries tasted best from our neighbor's trees.
We climbed up on the neighbor's garage roof and did as we pleased.
In the evening, empty streets were special to us as others
Were called home for dinner by their frantic mothers.
Kick the car was our favorite pastime. We played alone
Until Mom had dinner on the table and called us home.
We played until the street lights came on then we gave in
Until the following day when we would kick the can again.
The Episcopal church was in a town five miles away.
But this was one of our favorite independent days.
We were dropped off by Dad on his way to buy a newspaper and tobacco.
Walking from church, stopped at a bakery, bought something special.
We also walked out to the Coyote Point Junior College swimming pool,
Wearing only our swimsuits and tennis shoes and carrying a towel.
Russian River rafting, hitchhiking to the beach, picking blackberries,
Skiing at Sugar Bowl, dancing with the college boys—happy memories.
When I met my first husband in San Francisco, my brother came along.
Off I went to Laguna Beach to join my friends with my brother's approval.
At 18, with Tom's love, and my independence, I was ready to marry Karl.

Brenda and older brother Tom Thompson, 1958.

One Bar

Is it possible for a family of six to share
One family bathroom with only one bar
Of soap for washing the hair?
Looking back, I scarcely believe it is true.
This was before the advent of shampoo.
Palmolive soap is all we had.
When it was my turn to bathe
Just getting the bathroom made me glad.
One bar of soap washed me from head to toe.
We had no TV so I didn't know
All the finer things in life were outside our door.
Having the bath to myself, I didn't ask for more.
No luxury shampoo; no conditioner either.
For me that just made for less of a bother.
As long as the bar of soap was there,
I could wash my body and even my hair.
Everyone had a specific bath time.
Early in the morning before school was mine.
Each one had a bathing routine.
One bar of soap kept us all clean.

In the Fair

Have you ever entered in the County Fair?
Not simply just attending, but being there?
I entered a pie once but forgot the salt.
It looked really good but it was not.
My daughter showed her 4-H pig.
She was small. The pig was big.
Herding a pig is not an easy thing.
With a cane she guided the pig
Skillfully around the showcase ring.
I never jumped a frog in the inner circle.
That was for those who were really skillful.
I wonder if Mark Twain had ever known
That a jumping frog would steal the show.
I entered the "Belle of the Camp" competition.
Older ladies were asked to tell ol' stories
Of Calaveras County's early glories.
I made an outfit and did some research.
I told of the bells in the oldest church.
The bells are amazing but no one really cared to hear
Of my story and the historic bells that year.
It was so much fun, the next year I tried again.
I told of Belle in "Beauty and the Beast."
It was a popular Disney movie that year.
I made Belle the heroine of our camp.
It was a hit, and won the honor of the win.
Being part of the county fair made me glad I entered again.

Belle of the Camp.

Chasing Cows

Remembering Summers with Sonia

The summer campground sits peacefully along the river.
High Sierra open-range cattle roam freely along the banks.
Early morning brings wandering cows for a drink,
Leaving cow pies all over the land.
The gentle clang of the cowbells gives warning.
Once again, the cows must be chased away.
The morning cow chase begins again.
A young woman dances gaily from stone to stone
Waiving a willow branch to ward off the intruders,
Protecting the campsite for another day.
A small child joins in the morning ritual.
She stands alone against an advancing cow.
Legs set firm in a challenging stance, she confronts
The lumbering intruder as it comes into sight.
Waving a stick, she lets out a holler,
"Don't poop here, Poop Cow!"
The marauding cow wanders off.
The campfire is lit. The coffee perks. Once again
All is peaceful in the High Sierra campground.

Marvelous Friend, Norman Prigge

Did you know you are my marvelous friend?
Quite extraordinary and special to me!
Without you my life would be quite ordinary—
And I'm still searching for a reason just to be.
We may not think alike or enjoy all the same things,
But when you smile at my jokes my heart sings.
Knowing you has added so much pleasure;
You are a marvelous friend beyond measure.
I've had wonderful lifetime friends in the past,
And I thought those friendships would ever last.
Then came aging and distances apart.
Now those friendships are only in my heart.
But you, my marvelous ever-constant friend,
Shall be with me till the end.
Each calendar day goes drifting by,
Each rising sun and evening star;
Yet the time we spend quells my search
For this reason we have come this far.

Norman, this is for you. You are indeed my special, marvelous friend.
Love, Brenda

Don't Tell Sam

Nothing is perfect at our house.
The roof's got a leak and the door's got a squeak.
And a crow drops its business on Sam's car.
I try to cheer Sam up when things don't go right.
I just remind myself, "Don't tell Sam."
When the window washers don't come,
And the tree trimmer cuts the wrong limb,
I try to remain calm and don't tell Sam.
Blustery weather blows ashes on Sam's car
Reminding one fire danger is not very far.
I quake in my boots, but don't tell Sam.
The waiter forgets the salt and pepper shaker.
Sam's evening meal is often over dry
While mine is perfect. I don't know why.
I enjoy his company and quick repartee.
Things that bother him, just don't bother me.
To keep the peace and have fun, I don't tell Sam.
To air my views on political strife and civil unrest,
I really don't know what is best;
To explain to him just who I am
Or just keep quiet and not tell Sam.

I Remember Goldia Schuck

I didn't know what to expect as I drove this little elderly woman home from church one Sunday. All I knew was that she lived in an old grocery store and needed a ride home. The front of the store was just two huge glass windows set in an old stone building overlooking the main street in Mokelumne Hill. In the rear of the building she had a small apartment. The space was just large enough for a small bedroom, a small bath, and an equally small kitchen; just big enough for this petite lady.

Goldia Schuck was a survivor. An amputee from childhood, Goldia had one good leg and an old wooden one that got her around pretty well. Small and gentle, she observed the world from one of the front windows that allowed her to see the comings and goings on the street. Directly across the street was the town post office.

Goldia was very resourceful. She kept a quilting frame in the back of the large front room and kept a piecing basket next to her chair. She used old fabric that told the history of her life. Although she used a wheelchair, she never strayed far from her window and quilting.

So why was she so interested in me? Sure, I could give her a ride to and from church but it was more than that. She heard I was looking for a location to set up a small real estate office. So she had an idea. Several years before, Goldia had served the community of Mokelumne Hill as their librarian. She had no education and no library experience. She just loved people, particularly the children. Her spacious front room overlooking the main street in Mokelumne Hill was the perfect location for a small library. Now the county was taking the library away. They told her they needed a licensed librarian. The storefront was soon empty of books. Goldia missed the people coming in for books and seeing the children. I was amazed that she thought I could help her. She proposed that I rent one half the store front for an office. Soon, couples and families were stopping by to investigate real estate investment possibilities in the area and I was in business. What a surprise and what a wonderful partnership we began.

I was with Goldia in that location until her death. She made an impression on all who met her. In addition to her quilting business, she sewed clothing for my daughter. She even made the evening gown my daughter wore when she ran for Miss Calaveras. I never saw her use a sewing machine. Everything was sewn by hand.

She outlived her husband and daughter by at least thirty years. She outlived her friends as well. To me, she was part of my family and I shall never forget her.

Brenda's friend, Goldia Schuck.

Visiting Grace

Country roads lead to secret places.
Pavement turns to dirt paths no longer used by local inhabitants.
The centuries-old rustic fence still surrounded the cemetery.
A rusty old gate hung loosely on its remaining hinges.
It creaked as I pushed it through the overgrown grass and weeds.
I was afraid it might fall off the drooping old post.
Things were looking bad enough without me making things worse.
An ancient oak spread its canopy of leaves and shielded the graves.
The shade the tree offered seemed to welcome me.
An old bench still sat upright. I prayed it would hold my weight.
It was necessary to sit a moment to gather my thoughts.
Was this the place? The last destination of my friend Grace?
I knew her decade-old family history was buried there.
Would I be able to sense her spirit? Envision her face?
All was silent. A gentle breeze kissed my cheek.
I smiled, believing my friend had welcomed me there.

Amy Marries Isabeau

Two spirits have come together in love.
They are asking for blessings from above.
A Caribbean beauty is standing tall
Embracing the moment in front of all.
A forever-young Amy stands by her side
Her face is aglow with marital pride.
Joining Isabeau and Amy was meant to be
In a joyous marriage by the shining sea.
The family celebrates this joining of two—
Forever may their vows remain new.
Our hearts are filled with love and we pray
That everyone here on this joyous day
Will remember with special family pride
All that we hold unspoken, kept inside,
That expresses a world breaking free
Shining a radiant light as life is meant to be.
The Thompson family is richer for this expression
Of boundless love we are privileged to witness.

Then Came a Raft

A summer hike down an unknown canyon to Natural Bridges on the creek leading to the Stanislaus River seemed like a good adventure for me and my twin six-year-old grandsons. Not knowing what lay ahead, I wandered along down the steep path with both boys in tow. Ever aware of the poison oak that crept onto the dirt trail from both sides, I kept thinking I really should have put long pants on myself and the boys. I questioned if this adventure was going to end up a disaster. Sure hoped I had some Fels-Naptha soap left over from last summer's poison oak episode. We were certain to have some of the oil on our legs before the day was out. Knowing a good washing usually saved the day, I gave in to the inevitable.

Halfway down the trail, I began to worry about the long climb up that awaited us. It was getting hotter and I had neglected to bring water. Who knew a two-mile hike could be so long or steep? So down the path we went. When the path gave us a choice of directions, we chose the one that looked like it was going straight down the canyon. We didn't want to accidentally double back up to our parked car. Seems like we chose correctly, as soon the sparkling creek leading to the river was in sight. What a relief!

Now, instead of poison oak, we had giant granite boulders to contend with. My knees weren't used to climbing. Once again, I questioned my ability to search out safe adventures with my grandchildren. They were having great fun. Climbing down the trail and up and over rocks was what they loved most. The bad part for me was the knowledge that at the end of the day, sore legs and all, I was going to have to hike up and out of the canyon.

Upon reaching the creek, with the wondrous lava bridge, I was both amazed at the beauty and thrilled by the accomplishment of getting there. The Natural Bridges arched gracefully over a large dark pond leading up the canyon. I had no idea how far up the creek the pond reached or how wide the bridge was. The dark pond had water dripping from ancient stalagmites and in one place the water cascaded into the pond from a fissure in the lava rock. It was rather inviting in a mysterious way. It was dark in the cave. How deep was the water? How deep was the cave? I didn't know anyone who had ever been down to see it before. We waded in up to our ankles and stood pondering the wisdom of going deeper in the water. I could see a slight glimpse of light reflecting on the pond deep inside. The huge cavern must have an exit, I thought.

Quite unexpectedly, a woman and her children emerged from the cave. Out they came, floating on a large blowup raft. One even hung on to the back of the raft and kicked vigorously to move the raft along. The mother and her small children were perfectly relaxed and having a great time. What a great way to explore the pond! As we stood there envious of the chance to explore the cavern and the pond, the young woman and her children disembarked and came walking over. To our amazement, she offered us the use of her raft. "It's the only way to experience Natural Bridges," she declared. She said she came often and was happy to splash in the creek while we took a ride on the raft. As had happened so many times in my life, I couldn't express my gratitude enough. People in Calaveras County are so generous and kind. We floated through the cave and came out on the other side. There is no way we could have entered the pond without the raft. Knowing the cave wasn't filled with unknown terrors was a great relief.

I've never made that hike again. Sometimes I see cars parked up on the road at the trailhead. I always wonder if someone told them to bring a raft.

The Daughter

As the oldest daughter, I stood alone
Guarding my thoughts and feelings.
Now, my daughter seeks my advice
To help give her spinning life meaning.
Have I learned any lessons in life?
I'm quite unaware of her personal strife.
Is it possible for me to sympathize
With the problems I see when I look in her eyes?
I have no idea of the torment she feels
Because to me her struggles appear unreal.
As the eldest daughter, I led an independent role,
Never allowing my emotions to show.
Now, I try to imagine her struggle in life.
Was there ever a time I was that vulnerable?
Perhaps, when wounded, I buried my pain;
I found it easier than trying to explain.
When my wonderful daughter confides in me,
I wish my council could set her heart free.
Now, I try to stand strong as I did when I was young
Yet I feel her complex life is not like my own.
Being a young woman is being alone in the world
And the difficulties one must surmount are unique.
Oh, that I had the answers to all that she confides
To put her mind at rest and allow her to sleep.

My Son

A woman is celebrated when she gives birth to a son.
So I was quite thrilled when I had one.
Born on his German grandfather's birthday
Made him special in so many ways.
The father of my son was also an only son and he
Was expected to carry on the family tree.

My son Chris's early days were different from most.
Living in Europe, he lived through my turbulent divorce.
My parent-in-laws loved my children and were always near.
They supported my decisions and were always there
Offering love and granting us much needed care.

Returning to California, a loving family was the goal
Along came Barry Young to fill the father role.
Barry put a new balance in our lives—his children, a surprise.
We experienced a complicated life we had not visualized.
Now, there were six children instead of two.
I did the best I could with a situation quite new.

Then, off to college and an independent life,
A new career, a new home and a beautiful new wife.
With great determination, he overcame the family drinking disease.
He displayed a new strength and put his family at ease.
Now, a strong husband, father and grandfather we see
The wonderful man he was always meant to be.

Family Tradition

When Saint Paul said, "For now we see through a glass darkly," he wasn't kidding. So little of what happens all around us is not registered in our brains in a fashion from which we can learn. When I was young, and most of my life, I have "thought like a child," a passage also attributed to Paul. Now, in my mid-eighties, I am beginning to get some insight and understanding of some unseemly behavior.

While dining with my niece and her eighteen-year-old daughter, I ordered a fancy alcohol drink. With strawberries, as I recall. My niece thought it sounded good and she ordered one too. Then she asked her eighteen-year-old if she would like one also. I was kind of puzzled. We were celebrating the girl's first year at college. It was a joyous moment. But the drinking age in California is twenty-one. I reflected briefly that I was drinking at eighteen, but my mother wasn't buying the drinks. My first thought was that the restaurant could lose its license. That's certainly something one thinks of at an older age. Luckily, the waiter asked the girl for her I.D. However, that wasn't the end of it. My niece tried to insist by stating her daughter had left her purse at home. I was relieved when that didn't work. In a college town, I think they have heard that old ruse before. I must admit, drinking outside the law would not be so much fun for me if we were caught.

Then, I had a moment to reflect. When my daughter was nineteen, she was on her way to France for a year in the Bordeau wine region to enhance her Enology degree. I thought it would be great to have a drink with my daughter before she flew off. We decided to drive to a Mexican restaurant in the neighboring county. So what would be better than to drink margaritas to celebrate. My daughter had brought her own car. She drove a Fiat convertible. She had her six-foot-tall boyfriend with her. Was he even twenty-one? I don't recall. I remember that she rolled the car in a ditch on the way home. Children aren't infallible. But thank God they are protected by guardian angels. The boy ended up in a neck brace for months. My daughter survived unscathed and went off to France. I did feel responsible after the accident. My daughter wasn't a drinker. Giving hard liquor to a minor isn't just a bad idea, it's terribly dangerous.

Somehow, I lived through some very crazy times outside the law. At eighteen, I got a job working in a ski resort. At night, we all hung out in a beer garden in the ski lodge. I looked older and no one ever carded me. That is to say no one ever asked for a photo I.D. We danced and drank until the beer garden closed at two in the morning. It never affected our skiing. Life was just one big holiday. My mother came to visit and was concerned for me. She knew I wasn't a heavy drinker. I just had a beer to fit in with the ski crowd. But mom, didn't want me to be arrested either. So she falsified a birth certificate for me. Amazing but true. Mom worked at the county courthouse in the clerk's office. I can't imagine what she was thinking. She could have lost her job. Our family was not well situated. She couldn't afford to lose her job. But she took a risk for me. Looking back, it all seems impossible. Must be some kind of family tradition. A dangerous rite of passage.

Family Reunion

We shall sail away to that distant shore
And see those we thought we'd see no more.
Will they have aged the same as we?
Will they really know that it's me?
I have missed those dear to my heart
I hardly recall how long we've been apart.
Family, old friends and husbands too,
Even friends that are fairly new
Have gone quietly on before
And on this Earth are seen no more.
We will surely meet again and claim
Our loves, our families without shame.
Old troubles and squabbles will be left behind
We will be met with a love sublime.
For surely such love ever felt shall not die
Nor fade like photos of days gone by.
A glorious reunion awaits at lives' end.
We will love and talk and begin again.
There is so much I want to say—
It will have to wait for our reunion day.

Smitten

To love and be loved is a dream.
To have someone to love is my goal.
Being loved is not all it seems;
I prefer the man I conjure in my dreams.
He may not even know my name.
But I am smitten by him all the same.
Some would say I have a teenage crush.
A "youthful love" just makes me blush.
When I encounter him my heart beats fast.
Can such a teen-age passion last?
I care not for what tomorrow brings
Seeing him approach my heart sings.
Dreams of passionate days in my past
Will make the fantasy warm and last.
This state of temporal euphoria,
Is all I crave just a little more of.
Perhaps its best not to speak or say
My thoughts would only drive him away.

Brenda enjoying a hike in nature.

Surrounded by Nature

Early Stirrings

The brown bear stirs in his hollow log.
The forest creatures snuggle up for warmth.
Small birds stay hidden in their winter nests.
The damp ground holds new growth concealed.
Bits of sunlight warm the misty air.
Small green shoots look for an opening
Between the leaves on the wet winter floor.
Our restless hearts stir for companionship
And warm smiles from friends.
Like sodden leaves pressed down on the cold earth
Our smiles are concealed behind our masks.
We feel the dampness in our bones
For lack of human warmth and daily greetings.
Soon the sunlight will cause Mother Nature to surprise us.
Our pleasure may be all that she can bring.
Green shoots awaiting the warmer days.
The bear will emerge into the sunlight.
Take strength knowing in time we too shall emerge.

Not Time Yet

They say there is a time for everything under heaven.
The garden is sprouting from the last winter storm.
The air is cold but the sun is warm.
I want to start working in my garden.
But it's not time yet.

My winter clothes look like they need to go.
There is no longer need to prepare for the snow.
Somewhere, I saved last summer's clothes.
I could wash them and get them out.
But it's not time yet.

Summer vacation can't be far off.
All kinds of bargains are on my iPhone.
Can't think of a reason I need to stay home.
I could book plans for a stay and a plane.
But it's not time yet.

I'll make a list of all I have to do.
Some things can wait. Others I need to attend.
Really, no rush, as Spring is not here again.
I'm my own worst taskmaster.
I just need to slow down. I have plenty of time.

May Roses

May is the month for roses
I walk through the garden and see
New buds surrounding me.
The winter has seemed long this year
And I'm happy for the blooms of spring.
Although I walk often in the garden,
I hadn't noticed the tiny buds appearing.
And now, they burst forth in bloom.
Was it longer sunlight that caused the bloom?
Was it the gentle warming of the earth?
The first rose is always an unexpected surprise.
I sit and observe the other buds
And admire their unique beauty.
A butterfly drifts by. The air is still.
I celebrate the perfect day in May.

Photo by Author.

Escape

A quiet solitude encompasses me.
The stillness offers me a momentary peace.
A small bird hops on a leafless branch.
Not a sound is heard. All is as it has been.
Away from the cities and crowds
My heart takes comfort in silence.
My mind wanders off to a different place.
I close my eyes and imagine a peaceful shore
Where waves wash the sun-drenched sand.
A smile crosses my lips. Like the small bird I am set free.
The splashing waves now speak to me.
Set loose, I sail away to a forgotten land.
The rolling ocean calls my name.
In silence, I slip away to a distant space.
Sand castles and sea birds await me.
White clouds, drenched in sunlight,
Float above to new horizons.
Like a kite I soar and join the floating clouds.

August Heat

The sun is hot in the sky above
Not an afternoon for making love.
The sandy shore retains the heat.
Burning dog's paws and my bare feet.
The early summer fog is lifted
At last, a sunny summer day is gifted.
Now for the August heat.

The sun sits in the burning sky.
The little birdbath is almost dry.
I thank God for the leafy shade.
It's no place to be out today.
Air-conditioning makes me shiver.
I wish I was down at the river
Celebrating the August heat.

Now the flowers begin to fade.
They have had their better days.
I still keep my routine of watering
The birds still flutter their dusty wings.
I'm always glad when the sun goes down.
The trees are slowly turning brown.
There's little relief from the August heat.

Riding to Hounds

First, let me state before I start,
While attending a fox hunt, one must look the part.
The clothes are a costume all their own.
Leave the spurs and chaps at home!
The dressmaker ordered Harris Tweed
For the sporting jacket I would need.
No jeans or cowboy boots would do.
I had to have special leather jumping shoes.
Jodhpur pants and a helmet were all brand new.
This outing was costing quite a few marks.
Riding in Germany was more than a lark.
The horses are used to the full-on gallop;
If you're not ready, you learn quickly to adapt.
At least twenty hounds were poised and ready;
The hound master had to keep them steady.
Let me state here that no fox was used…
That would admit to animal abuse.
The hound master rode out front with a drag bag
We followed quickly. No one could lag.
The yelping dogs led on in pursuit.
We rode all together in a raggedy group.
Some jumped the hedges, some cleared the wall,
I managed the gates and didn't jump at all.
At the finish, we gathered at a traditional country inn.
I wish I could do it all over again.

Autumn Expectations

I remember the beginning of school every year;
New clothes, new shoes, new books, pencils and binders,
Renewing friendships and looking forward to new friends.
I remember the smell of freshly mimeographed handouts.
We quickly scanned new textbooks for pictures and
Tried to imagine the new subjects that only the teacher knew.
We started out for school neat as a pin.
By lunchtime, it was too warm to wear the new sweater.
By the end of the week, our shoes were scuffed
And the new sweater was nowhere to be found.
Lunch in the cafeteria with the smell of macaroni and cheese.
Standing in line waiting for the next bell.
Then a whole new world of expectations—
Waiting to choose sides for baseball and field hockey.
Waiting to plan the Halloween activities. What to wear?
Awaiting the first rains and wondering where my umbrella was.
Wondering if the new boy would walk me to school.

Christmas Tree

While driving down a street into town one day
I spied a brightly lit Christmas tree along the way.
It was in a tenement building three stories high.
I saw it in a curtained window as I drove by.
The tree wasn't tall—not decorated well at all—
But it brought back memories I could recall
Of my youth and decorating the Christmas tree.
We had many a one-sided Christmas tree.
Some tall, some short, always rather skinny.
Dad would add a branch to an open bare spot
With silver tinsel hanging free so as not
To bring one's attention to lack of perfection.
The smell of cinnamon cookies in the air
Mom's cooking was the evening fare.
All over the world, whatever the reason,
We rejoice in the holiday season
And look for a decorated Christmas tree.
Merry Christmas!

Ode to a Poinsettia

What joy living plants bring
To an apartment without a garden.
No natural soil awaits a transplant.
No natural light from the window.
The flowering plant sits alone.
Bringing color and love to a home.

How kind someone was to send
This plant, seeking only water,
To create a pleasure till the end.
But then the end comes. Long
The blossoms have spread their joy.
Now, it's time for them to die.

No joy comes from the final blow.
Now is time for the plant to go.
The dying plant is taken into hand
And gently tossed into the trash can.
Would that it could find another life.
For a dying plant there is no demand.

One More Hour

Oh, that I might have one more day with you.
If not a day, then an hour or two.
My life bursts forth in a joyful dance—
Is this new feeling what is known as romance?
Days and hours drift by in an endless daze
Yet thoughts of you cause me to be amazed.
Our joy can be found in the simplest things.
Upon hearing your voice my heart takes wings.
Be with me and share a time without care.
Let not reason cause anxious hearts to linger
And destroy our precious moments together.
No fear- only joy. Let nothing stand in our way.
This can be the beginning or the end of our day.

The photo of the Japanese Tapestry is by author, 2018.

Travel Memories

Escaping the Mundane

We get up in the morning and open our eyes.
Few expectations. Just another day.
Then an idea springs into mind.
The mundane world is left behind.

Unlimited possibilities are there;
Wispy dreams hanging in the air.
Like billowing clouds set in a blue sky—
Our hopes and dreams appear far away.

We reach out in our imagination
Looking for meaning and light to shine
And inspire great action in a void of dreams,
 Giving action to the hopes within our minds.

Set your mind free of care; the answers are there.
Let happy memories flood the still air.
Endless travels of the mind set us free.
We do not need distant travel to see
What excites and fuels our minds are our own fantasies.

Author kicking back in Puerto Vallarta.

Old Photograph

I found an old photo of me.
The young girl I used to be.
The photo is in black and white—
Not a storm cloud in sight.
A picture on a trip to France
Showed me and at a glance
I could see I was very happy.
Many years have left their mark
On the girl pictured in the park.
France was so amazing then.
I remember those days and when
My new husband showed me the land
I was in his spell holding his hand.
The dress I wore was the best I had.
Being dressed-up in France made me glad.
I didn't speak French but Karl did
He was so sophisticated. I was just a kid.
Unfortunately, that marriage didn't last.
It's all part of a long ago past.
I remember that happy time when I see
The girl in the photo that I used to be.

Mariachis on My Mind

Our romantic hearts get lost in a dream.
They take us to places we've never seen.
Quiet evenings outdoors in a town square;
Hearing Mexican music just brings us there.
Like a certain movie background refrain,
The music awakens the dream again and again.
Sun drenched sands and palm trees come to mind—
And we leave all our mundane cares behind.
I imagine a quiet sunset, swimming in the glassy sea.
Romantic dreams of Mexico enrapture me.
In reality, it's not that far away.
There are many places where we can stay.
Still, the best places aren't easy to find.
First of all, the sprawling resorts come to mind.
Then, taking the time to look around,
We discover many small hotels in the older towns,
Really charming, if somewhat rundown.
I love the colorful people in the peaceful parks.
I imagine sitting quietly in the evenings dark
While my imagination fills in the story of a tale untold,
I become the star of my own movie yet to unfold.

Desert Life

Temperatures drop and the desert breathes again.
Oncoming winter holds promises of new life
And off-road travel adventures soon to begin.
Canadian "Snowbirds" head south in their vans.
The winter months in the Sonoran Desert are grand.
The small green Oasis, surrounded by palms,
Hides a desert blue fish along its sheltered banks.
Evenings, mountain sheep come down for cool water.
Early morning light reveals coyotes and rabbits
As well as chuckwallas and the illusive desert tortoises.
By noon, life slows down long enough to beat the lingering heat.
Then early evening shadows awaken a new life in the desert.
Vagabond strollers and children enjoy the colorful sunsets
Reaching from the brilliant west to the distant eastern horizon.
The quiet is broken only by the sound of off-road machines
That have roamed the desert to search out new scenes.
In spring the wildflowers will once again bloom.
For now, I shall treasure the photos I have in my room.

House on Stilts

I set forth in an old Jeep with my son and a guide up a narrow mountain trail to visit a primitive village in the northern hills of Thailand. I was celebrating my 74th birthday with an adventure outing. Surrounded by coffee plantations and dense bamboo forests, my guide, my son, and I arrived at a simple wooden house on stilts. It was at least six feet above the road. I asked the guide why the house sat up so high, as clearly there was no flood plain to contend with on top of a mountain.

"The reason the house sits so high up," he explained, "Is that the animals—cows, pigs, dogs and chickens—can night under the house for safety and warmth. Wild cats and snakes are common in the surrounding wooded areas."

Steep stairs led to the flooring of the small wooden house. There was no railing on the stairs. There were no interior walls inside the house…only woven curtains. The houses in the surrounding village were all of the same construction (although one ingenious owner had truck tires piled up for his stairs). The interior had neither plumbing or running water. A fairly good-sized outhouse stood fifty feet behind the house.

Inside the outhouse was a reservoir for holding water for washing and all other household needs. There is a cement slab in the center with a hole for bodily functions. It gives a new meaning to the need to have good balance to be able to squat. As there is limited lighting, I was given a small flashlight in case I needed to go out at night.

I'm sure the surrounding houses all used the same well I had seen when I first arrived. Firewood was neatly stacked under the houses where the animals slept. During the day, I saw women come up the canyon with baskets of kindling wood on their backs like backpacks. I didn't see any horses or donkeys. I guess there wasn't enough fodder that high up the mountain to feed much livestock.

All went well until night came. A primitive meal was provided by the homeowner on a wood-burning fire in a fire pit inside the house. Since the house is mostly open, smoke is not an issue. The fire pit had a concrete bowl to set it apart from the wood flooring. I didn't eat much as I wasn't accustomed to the spices.

Nevertheless, halfway through the night I needed to make a trip to the outhouse. There was no outside lighting. Don't those people go at night? Thank God for the light of the moon. My little flashlight wasn't of much use. I made it out, barefoot, without an injury. I didn't wake the people or their animals (or disgrace myself).

Once I was finished, I went back up the steep stairs into the house and carefully parted my mosquito netting and flopped down on my mattress. I heard a wind chime tingle in the evening breeze. I thanked God for my safety. Neither my son nor the guide commented the next day. I'm sure they must have heard me but no one said anything. However, the guide handed me the flashlight later that day stating it had been found in the outhouse and I needn't worry about returning it.

Brenda in Thailand.

Mountain Refuge—Ocean Escape

A quiet solitude surrounds me. The stillness promises peace.
A small bird hops on a leafless branch. Not a sound is heard.
All is as it has been. The mountains hide their age-old secrets.
Lake shores and rivers reflect the morning light.

Away from the cities and crowds, my heart takes comfort.
Then, my mind wanders off to a different place in time.
I close my eyes and imagine a life I once knew
Where waves crash onto the sun-bleached sand.

A smile crosses my lips. Like a bird set free, I fly to that distant land.
The ocean calls out my name. In silence, I soar above the waves.
Sand castles and sea birds await. The sparkling sea speaks to my past.
White clouds drenched in sunlight drift off to the horizon.

Now, the mountains have set me free. The ocean escape awaits.
I feel the drift of a current beneath the boat from days gone by.
I hear you call my name, in love, awaiting a glorious afternoon.
The sea swells as does my heart—remembering.

Then, once again, the present is nearby. I smell the pines.
A cooling breeze whispers softly caressing my skin.
Nature has once again seized me in its grasp.
I fill my lungs with its bounteous gift.

Steal Away

Steal away on the Iron Horse pacing slowly up the valley.
What better way to sip wine and visit Napa's beauty?
Leisurely snaking through fields of mustard flowers in the sun
The journey on the Napa Wine Train has just begun.
The train creeps along—never fast. Through fields in bloom
And grapevines, like an artist's watercolor from the past.
Nature's abundant grape harvest is yet to be.
The train surges forth on its tireless journey.
Excited tourists of all ages enjoy the scenic ride
While a wide variety of food and wine is tasted inside.
Lumbering along with views of the valley and the rolling hills
The little train moves, carefully assuring that no wine spills.
After a small breakfast, the train stops and all disembark.
Touring the wineries is like being in a manicured park.
Then back on the waiting train and wine tasting again.
At the end of the ride, many special moments are locked inside.
Meeting new voyagers, all happy from tasting good wine,
Reminds us of elegant days of train travel in a forgotten time.

Life in the Tropics

Life in Costa Rica is not like anything I had ever seen—
Seasides and volcanic hillsides—everything very green.
Our eyes feast on parrots, assorted monkeys in the trees,
Caiman, crocodiles, and turtles that come from the seas.
Over all the country, we see little houses in many colors,
That create a colorful painted landscape like no other.
Small houses painted red, yellow, blue, green—
Sometimes two colors and every shade in between.
I wonder where they got such vibrant paint.
The balance of color made the villages quaint.
Native trees and gardens take the place of city fences.
The surrounding lush green tropical forest is very dense.
With a diet of rice and beans, no need to go to the store.
No need to purchase extras as they lack for nothing more.
All kinds of tropical fruit and streams of fish complete the meal.
An occasional local chicken dish keeps the variety real.
The children are seen playing outside, rain or shine,
Everywhere soccer fields and plenty of trees to climb.
The quiet village life we saw as we passed through
Was serene and expressed a lifestyle to me quite new.
Frequent buses filled with tourists go rolling through.
Without tourism and agriculture, there isn't much to do.
Costa Rica is a peaceful country undaunted by worldly care.
I might feel abandoned by the world if I lived there.

Costa Rica, 2022.

The Pumpkin

Planning for travel to a foreign land
Limited what I could take in hand.
The airplane had a luggage limit.
I was supposed to stay within it.
Fodors is a travel guide
With useful hints tucked inside.
What to wear, how to pack,
All the things to be brought back.

I planned my trip to the "T"
No extra luggage would be with me.
Then a suggestion for Japan
Inspired ideas for that foreign land.
Small gifts are often given to show
Friendship to strangers on the go.
Business cards and photos of home
Showed others we're not alone.

The world is such a small place
These small gifts seem to connect our race.
Because children are so much fun,
I thought I'd bring gifts for some.
I had no idea what to do. Would you?
It had to be something new.

I went to the travel bureau in our town.
I knew they wouldn't let me down.
They had postcards and folded fans—
Small gifts I could pack for Japan.
Colorful stickers caught my eye
I thought I would give them a try.

With pictures from my hometown
Where Mark Twain gained renown
For his story of a jumping frog contest
When the town was the wild wild west.
The little stickers would be a success.
For little children, it was the best.

I sat on a bench in the parks in Japan
And became a curio from a foreign land.
Children and parents alike stopped to see
The foreign woman. That was me!
I handed out the stickers till they were gone.
They were a success with everyone.
Who would have guessed stickers could be so much fun?

Then one small boy ran off to his family
And returned with a surprise gift for me.
In his little hand an orange pumpkin.
A happy memory from a happy land.
I shall never forget Japan.

The pumpkin sits with other treasures
On a shelf reserved for such pleasures.
The precious smiles are easy to recall.
Gifts from the heart are long-lasting, after all.

Wild European Adventure

Norm had planned this trip in advance.
It was a wild adventure at very first glance.
Three countries back-to-back in a continuous line.
Covid had made a mess of the original time.
The tour company had booked all three—
First France then Spain, Portugal, and Italy.
Brenda decided it would be fun to go.
She wanted to see the Dolomites without snow.
Norm and Brenda had traveled together before
Three tours in Europe were but one adventure more.
First to see France in April, and the Loire,
Then Spain, Italy, and one country more.
Around the French castles they did go
With an energetic group they didn't know.
Cobblestones were on all the streets.
How tired they were—dead on their feet!
An evening soak in a gigantic bathtub,
Then a massage with a good foot rub.
The next day they were at it again.
Completing 50 days since they began.
All the European sights did amaze.
Something they will treasure the rest of their days.

A Dress for Martha

At a country school in Costa Rica,
Surrounded by students, Martha stood alone, sad and shy.
I couldn't really see into her mysterious dark eyes.
She held her head and shoulders humbly down.
She shuffled her shoes on the dusty playground.
School buildings surrounded by tropical trees,
Were primitive and let in the gentle breeze.
No windows, no doors, more like a shed,
Yet tables, chairs, blackboard and books to be read.
Just one teacher and a principal to govern the school.
Children walked for miles—no buses or carpool.
The children attend classes fit for seven to seventeen
With regular courses and sports in between.
Martha took my hand and showed me around
The two classrooms and the playground.
Since tourists donate and add a financial benefit,
We were welcomed with a small musical event.
Three older girls had colorful skirts and danced.
Because they had the outfits, they were given a chance.
I asked Martha if she liked to dance. She smiled and nodded.
I knew she would readily welcome the chance if afforded.
I asked her where a girl could get such a colorful dress.
"It must be from the school," was her best guess.
I spoke to the principal and bought her a dress that day.
A little Honduran refugee gave meaning to my Costa Rican stay.

Martha in her new dress, Costa Rica, 2022.

Three Generations - 2021:
Brenda with her granddaughter Sonia Hiller and great-granddaughter Hadley.

History in the Making

Wild Times—Did Anyone Work?

The flapper-age roared in on a blazing stage.
Long Island wild parties were all the rage.
Flamboyant exuberance spilled over high society.
Luxurious galas quite foreign to you and me.

Jazz time brought the Roaring '20s out of hand.
Even though prohibition of alcohol was in our land.
The people drank without a care.
Private parties sprung up everywhere.

Bathtub gin, rum, and whiskey could be found—
One needed only look around.
Books are written about that time.
Wild parties made it seem sublime.

Although the booze was quite illegal,
That didn't stop the partying people.
All that was in the '20s forbidden,
Was quite ingeniously hidden.

F. Scott Fitzgerald celebrated the craze;
With books, parties, and rode the wave.
Movies glamorize that riotous time.

Our present lives are so much simpler.
The lost decade faded without a whimper.
Social consciousness makes us aware.
No more drinking and driving without care.

Alcohol and drugs are more discreet.
We are aiming for a goal we can meet.
The flapper days are long gone.
Not to say all-night parties were wrong!

Times have changed. Bars have closed.
What the future holds, no one knows.
We live in a world we never imagined.

Artificial intelligence makes us obsolete.
In the future, what will we drink and eat?
Wine bars are a civilized meeting place.
We sit and sip without haste.

Yet where is the cool hot jazz?
Where is the razzamatazz?
Are we left with a sterilized land?
Not even a red-hot Dixieland band?

Put me on a rocket to the moon.
Life will be over way too soon.
But place a glass of vodka in my hand.
I may need a drink in that faraway land.

I'll play music on my iPhone
And broadcast it on my Bose.
What I'll find on the moon,
God only knows.

Soiree

Modernism and nostalgia collided between wars in France.
Paris was a magnet for individual expression.
The Lost Generation ushered in a new world of art.
In the drawing rooms of the wealthy, they gathered—
Writers, artists, poets, and the existentialists.
On Saturdays, Gertrude Stein held soirees for her friends.
Hemingway, Scott Fitzgerald, Matisse, Picasso and others.
The ebullient society ate and drank and shared ideas.
Paris celebrated and encouraged these new talents
Pablo Picasso was promoted and supported by Stein.
Her close friend, Alice B. Toklas, cooked and entertained.
In some societies, "Friends of Friends aren't welcome,"
But that wasn't the case at Stein's Saturday gatherings.
The door was open and Stein's soirees were the center
Of an ever growing and exploding world of expression.
How wonderful it must have been to meet the artist,
Hear the stories behind the art and share a glass of wine.
Two American women living creatively in their own time
Added to the female freedom of sexual experience and
Gave all of Paris literati something new to talk about.

Snake Driving

Patrick drove snakes from Ireland, they say.
I think about this on St. Patrick's Day.
But I wonder about this. How can it be?
One man drove the snakes out to the sea?
He must have been a very lucky guy
Not to get even one bite
Before the snakes were out of sight.
No wonder Ireland made him a saint—
If ever there was a reason, this is one.
He got sainted when it was done.
If only someone could make all snakes flee,
What a superhero he would be.
Irish luck blessed that distant land.
Let's pray that a Patrick shows up here.
Too many snakes are crawling around.
And it is more than crawling snakes we fear.
One blessed man or woman is all we need.
Pray God grants us it comes with speed.
We don't need to wish on a four-leaf clover.
Just wake me up when the election is over.

MLK Jr.

The world was still reeling from the death of the Kennedy brothers.
Was it really possible for the senseless death of another?
Not knowing of the legendary leadership of Martin Luther King,
Could this targeted violence be the end for all that he had been.
We knew Martin had stood strong in a land that had gone wrong.
Racial injustice, fair housing, available health care and desegregation
Were only some of the huge social issues inflaming the nation.
One dedicated black man's voice rose above all others;
He spoke to all of our nation's poverty, not only his brothers.

While supporting the sanitary worker's right to strike,
He offered America an awareness that his march made right—
Defining The Poor People's campaign on that fatal night.
Joined by civil rights workers in his dogged campaign,
Spreading equal rights for all women and men was his aim.
With the world for his church, this eloquent preacher
Spoke to America as our relentless civil rights teacher.
One dedicated black man's voice rose above all others.
Martin spoke of all our nation's poverty, not only our brothers.

Martin Luther King Jr. died April 4, 1968.

Land of the Free

I've traveled abroad to foreign lands,
I've met people of all kinds
Wondering what is on our minds.
The land of the free where violence stands.
My first great trip across the sea
Was November 24, '63—
Two days after the murder of John F. Kennedy.
Our innocent minds went numb
Nothing prepared us for what was to come.
In '68 we lost MLK and then Bobby
How do you reply? I'm often asked.
Our valiant history stands on its own.
Over five hundred years of struggle
And our great America is still our home.
Let's consider the world's rocky past—
Invasions and intrigue have been the norm
Long before I was born.
Books have been written to try to explain
A dictator's rule, a monarch's reign.
My reply to all will ever be the same.
America is where I want to be.
I'm proud to live in America—the Land of the Free.

What Next?

While quietly enjoying an afternoon nap,
I remember when I held grandchildren on my lap.
Squirming grandchildren wanting to play
And wanting to escape my arms in any way
They could to break my loving grip.
Wanting to climb and give me the slip.
Now, I have great-grandchildren, as well.
Being with them makes my heart swell.
They are the future I will never know.
Still, I watch all my grandchildren grow.
Some are my own blood—some God gave me.
They are the future, whatever that may be.
Can they ever be prepared for what life has in store?
I can give them love and nothing more.
My aging heart breaks when I realize
They are growing up fast before my eyes
And this troubled world I will leave behind
Is not the safe place I wish them to find.
My belief in God and faith in the goodness of man
Is not something which they will understand
If wars continue to scorch this troubled earth.
May reason prevail and a new justice give birth.

Hiking trail in Puerto Vallarta.

The patio garden at The Meadows retreat home.

Bits and Pieces

The Red Purse

The silver-haired nonagenarian sits alone in the corner.
She observes from afar the room of chatting women.
She wonders, "Is this the end-life for women like me?"
She expects nothing from this "get-acquainted" gathering.
Once she dressed-up just to fit in and enjoy such a group.
Now, she sits by herself thinking of something to say.
Her once fashionable clothes are years out of date.
On her four-wheeled roller, sits a small leather purse.
The shining red leather is smooth and new looking.
The old leather purse reminds her of her glory days.
Unexpectedly, as she sits quietly, a woman approaches.
"Now, that is a fashion statement!" A woman declares,
As she spies the red purse just sitting there.
Such a small statement causes the woman to smile.
Her silent presence has been noticed after all.
The little red purse has stood the test of time.

The Purse.

Shy Boy

Jenny lived next door to Robert. They seldom saw one another as the building they lived in had strict shelter-in-place rules. There was a virus running rampant in their community and socializing was out of the question.

Robert was quite happy with the quiet days of no visitors. Life was very routine for him. Everything he did had purpose; an uninterrupted life with no variance. He got up each morning at the same time. Had the same thing for breakfast each day then washed and put his dish and silverware back in their proper place. Maybe he listened to classical music for an hour and read a good book. Maybe not. Working the *New York Times* crossword could also be a morning activity if he was lucky enough to find a newspaper in the lobby. Television was saved for late afternoon news and maybe an early movie. But every day was pretty much the same.

Jenny had a dog and her life was quite different. The dog determined her schedule. Living on the second floor of the retirement building, she had little choice but to get up early each morning with the sunrise and trudge outdoors to walk her dog, Blue. This meant going downstairs and out into the cold morning air as having a doggy door was a thing of the past. Living upstairs made walking the dog an ever-recurring activity. Then mid-morning Blue let her know it was time to go out again. Practically every four hours, the dog sat with a longing face needing attention. Jenny wondered if there wasn't an easier way to walk the dog but she appreciated that Blue kept her fit and out in the fresh air. Although she played bridge most afternoons for several hours, having walked the dog twice already gave her time to herself and the dog seemed to understand. The evening walk and stroll after dark were pretty much the regular routine for Jenny.

So where was the social life? Was one expected to shelter in place forever? It seemed so to both Jenny and Robert. Just about the time the death rate due to the ever-present virus seemed to lessen, a holiday came along and the virus reached a new level of contamination. Many people just disregarded the rules and gave up wearing a mask to be social once more. Living without human contact was just too much for most people. Robert and Jenny were fully aware of the dangers of socializing. An occasional hello in the hall was about the limit of their conversation for the first six months. Jenny could hear the television at times through the walls. "It's like living in the same house," she occasionally mused. "Rather like an old married couple who no longer talked much to one another."

Before long, Jenny realized fun and games would not be part of the life she had enjoyed in the past. She had enjoyed several marriages over the years and outlived all her previous partners. Now, having entered into her eighties, life had new meaning. Staying healthy was at the top of the list. It would be grand to have an adult conversation and a few laughs, but living a life without aches and pains was the best Jenny could wish for.

More and more she wondered what Robert did all day. She had seen into his apartment from the hall and knew he had fine furniture including a grandfather clock. She could hear the clock toll every hour and half hour, from inside her apartment. Again, it made her feel they were sharing the same space. She wondered if he was aware of her existence.

Blue could hear the comings and goings in the hall. He always barked at the lunch lady that daily rattled the trolley to Jenny's door and rapped rather loudly on it. Otherwise, the dog accepted the strange noises that occurred on a regular basis in the hall. Other dogs, repair men, and other tenants were of no interest to Blue. Jenny wondered if Blue and Robert would get along. Robert seemed to like the dog when they met in the hall. Blue was cautiously friendly. Perhaps a friendship was in the future.

Sometimes, Jenny imagined a conversation with her neighbor. Sometimes, she sang a song of her youth—an exhilarating feeling knowing no one could hear her raspy voice singing off-key. But mostly she wondered if Robert had hobbies or spent an inordinate amount of time on the computer.

As the year of the virus continued with no end in sight, Jenny resigned herself to an imaginary friendship with the shy boy next door. She began to treasure her imaginary friend to an extent that no real friendship could compare. She smiled at their new relationship.

And then one day he moved.

The Exit Door

Little Marybelle, with the fly-away hair, lived alone directly adjacent to the exit door of the retirement building. *Whoosh bang* the door slammed. The residents came and went continually; the front door of the retirement home was some distance from their rooms, so the exit door was the quickest way out of the complex.

She heard the door slam all day long. Lengthy halls wove throughout the complex leading to three floors of private apartments. She could see shadows of people through her curtains and hear muffled voices and occasional laughter as they walked away. But try as she might, she couldn't really discern the gist of their conversations. Because Marybelle moved into the home during the Coronavirus shelter-in-place regulation, she seldom saw anyone, much less make friends. She had not yet considered how much being entirely alone would affect her.

She herself didn't go out much. The restrictions of the Coronavirus weren't an extreme limitation for Marybelle. She was physically fit but her days of exploration were limited to necessary outings to the grocery store and doctor offices. When she turned 80 while living in her new apartment, she realized the retirement home embraced not only her new life, but the rest of her life. Marybelle had always enjoyed her old home. Life was good and she was content. She had few expectations of life and just enjoyed it as it came her way. But when her husband died after years of poor health, she was suddenly quite alone and had to reevaluate her future.

The first step was liquidating her assets. Selling her house took months. The whole process was rather traumatic for Marybelle; she had lived in the same house for almost 50 years. Downsizing and parting from her many years of accumulations was an ordeal. The large fine quality furniture was sold, left for the new buyer of the house, or given to family members. At first, family members wanted her to keep everything. "You can't sell that. It was grandma's!" protested her family. However, Marybelle knew she couldn't repurpose all the family possessions. Her new apartment was small and moving in was going to be a challenge.

The days following her husband's death, it became more and more evident to Marybelle it was time to move on. Every day presented itself with new questions she hadn't anticipated, nor did she didn't have any answers. There were so many new decisions to make. She didn't know anyone she could go to for advice. She had been independent for a long time and now daunting life decisions were hers alone to make. Settling her personal items was a bigger chore than she had imagined.

All the new furniture needed to be half the size of the old. The dining room furniture was sold with the house. (Few people had formal dining rooms anymore and her children were no exception.) The antique table and eight chairs, the mirrored buffet and sideboard, were all left for the new owners. Family members took very little. Marybelle was going to miss her days of entertaining.

The first day she moved into her new apartment, she heard a loud bang coming from outside, starling her. Marybelle wasn't used to the noise and had no idea what it was. But it happened again and again with a loud bang. *Whoosh bang.* She soon realized that it was the heavy exit door closing loudly.

It didn't take long for Marybelle to get over the initial shock. The bang was really not so loud and, although it occurred on a regular basis, she gradually became used to the sound. It became a daily anthem. Since she lived under the shelter-in-place restriction, it was practically the only sound she heard from the outside world. Like living near a railroad track, the daily sound became part of her world.

Marybelle lived a restricted life. Her meals were delivered to her room and she was encouraged not to go out. The virus that was running rampant in the world was also affecting friends and neighbors closer to the apartments. She wasn't very creative, so staying inside day after day caused Marybelle to reminisce about her past. She had some mementos on a bookcase to remind her of places and friends she recalled from days gone by. She sat in her new wing chair and gazed out the window. Her family came once and smiled and waved to her from the front lawn. But the visit didn't last long and wasn't very rewarding. They didn't come again.

Playing games on her computer and working jigsaw puzzles kept Marybelle entertained. Television and books rounded out her activities. Yet, the loneliness was pervasive. Somehow, the banging of the door reassured Marybelle she wasn't alone. How she longed for some casual conversation and a smile not hidden behind a mask. Often, she wondered what life was like outside her room. She knew that the regular ones coming and going were those with dogs to walk or the occasional resident out for a breath of fresh air. While Marybelle felt restricted in her confinement, she began to feel somewhat comfortable despite her isolation. At least she had the *whoosh-bang* of the exit door.

Then one day there was more banging and noise than usual outside her door. The heavy door was being replaced by a quiet one. Now, Marybelle truly felt cut-off from the world. The silence was deafening. The noise from the exit door had become her constant companion in the silence. She wondered how long until the shelter-in-place order would be lifted and life would take a turn for the better. She would make plans for the new person she would become. Maybe she would get a dog. She laughed at the memory of a door being her only companion.

A Halloween Tale

Autumn was in the air; and underfoot. The fallen leaves crunched under my new shoes as I walked to school. The smell of burning wood in my neighbor's fireplace and the chill in the air told me winter was on its way. My imaginary little brother ran ahead as I strolled along looking for my girlfriend, Gail. She was always late as she was very fussy about her hair, brushing it until it hung straight. Then, she didn't move her head for hours so every hair was in place. I was glad I had short brown curly hair that kind of did its own thing.

While Gail was busy with her hair, my imaginary brother kept me company on my early walks to school. His name was Marky. I named him after my dad, since my dad's name was Mark. Marky was better looking than most brothers. He was kind of short—about the same height as my mother. His hair was always tousled like mine—he probably had never seen a comb. Being a redhead, I always called him "carrot top" in my mind. Marky was always getting into trouble with my parents.

We were left alone a lot. I spent most of my time reading Nancy Drew mysteries. My imaginary brother did whatever he wanted and sometimes I got into mischief with him. One time he and I dressed up in my mother's clothes, high heels and all. One Halloween he was in for a big surprise. As Marky and I carefully put mom's clothes back in the closet, we discovered a box filled with Halloween costumes. Seems like Mom and Dad were going to a dress-up party. There was a Little Red Riding Hood costume and a wolf mask. Not what Marky had ever seen before. The wolf mask really caught his eye. It seemed to hold all the power and magic a young boy could imagine. He realized, with this scary mask he could frighten the wits out of all the girls at school, and maybe some boys.

The next day Marky tried the wolf mask out on Gail. He hid behind a bush and jumped out as we passed. Gail screamed and ran. The mask was a success. To make it scarier, Marky found an old dead rat and hung it from the rubber teeth of the wolf mask. It was gruesome. Marky ran about hiding in yards and alleys and jumping out at all and sundry. Marky had found his inner self. He loved his newfound power. He was particularly successful in the evening. Hiding in the shadow of a bush or tree, he would jump out and growl at some small kid and get a loud scream in return. I would sit in the house, reading a book and occasionally looking out the window, watching Marky terrorizing the neighborhood. But then things went bad.

A new boy moved in down the block. He was slightly older. He still went to our grammar school but he was older and had a bike he was allowed to ride to school. We didn't ever walk together. Then, I found out he had a bow and arrows. I wanted to warn him about Marky and the wolf mask, but it was too late. Marky hid behind a low stone wall one evening. Someone had placed pumpkins on the wall. The new boy thought the pumpkins made great target practice. There they were six carved pumpkins sitting on top of the wall. What great targets they made! Six pumpkins smiling out at the world. And before the boy could think, there was a wolf staring back at him.

So, of course, the boy let an arrow fly at the wolf behind the wall, and that was the end of Marky and the wolf. But you know, Marky wasn't real. I just imagined I had a little brother.

The new boy kind of took my imaginary little brother's place. He was full of mystery and adventure. For my next birthday I got a bicycle and soon became tired of Gail and her shiny straight hair. The new boy and I rode to school every day and I even learned to shoot a bow and arrow.

Post-It Note

A very nice lady invited me to tea.
When I asked a question, she replied TBD.
Was she sending me
A post-it note from her mind?
Could she not leave office speak behind?
"To Be Discovered" is clever speak.
It wasn't the answer I seek.
WTF I wanted to reply;
My anger was hard to deny.
Office shorthand is a good tool
But not for someone of the old school.
OMG I've heard my great-grandson say.
How do modern kids get that way?
What is wrong with using words?
Is language just for old ignorant nerds.
By the time I deciphered the letters
I forgot what I wanted to say.
I'll have to ask the nice lady another day.
I hope she leaves letter-talk at the office,
It would benefit the both of us.
Language is best in words spoken—
Then the conversation won't be broken.

Suffering

Can you imagine being thirsty? Really thirsty?
Can you imagine being hungry? Really hungry?
Can you imagine being lonely? Worried about safety?
Thinking your family would perish because of your blood?
Can you imagine being in fear of a world of hate
And keeping all your feelings locked inside?
Can you imagine your life of pain day by endless day?
Do you know what you would say, when asked?
"Do you think our lives will be OK?"
What are you going to say? What are you going to say?
Nothing in our lives prepares us for Hell on this earth.
What does it take to give the devil a new birth?
Without reason, our lives could be yanked aside.
We could be left naked with just our pride.
When Hell breaks loose, will we understand?
Could this Hell happen in our civilized land
One man's hate of another—can we honestly state
That we can foresee such an apocalyptic fate?
Nothing we can imagine begins to compare
With the Holocaust and what happened there.

Larger than Life

Some are put off by larger-than-life women.
How do I know? I may be one of them.
Julia Childs was over six feet tall.
Her stature took command over just about all.
Her undauntable spirit is what made her succeed.
She excelled in even the most ordinary deeds.
Julia wanted to be an agent for the good.
While working in France she excelled in great food.
She went undercover during the war
And served in a country she adored.
It was always her determination that set her apart
She had a feisty nature and a very kind heart.
We got to know her on her TV cooking show.
She taught us French words we didn't know.
The path to French cooking with a splash of wine
She taught me a skill for which I wasn't inclined.
Any cooking was a challenge when I was young,
But watching Julia's show made cooking seem fun.
I can still see her standing there with a glass of wine.
Her boldness never ceased to impress me every time.
She was a renaissance woman, it could be said.
She set the bar high with all that she did.

Nostalgia

My iPhone tells me nostalgia is defined as, "a sentimental longing or wistful affection for a return to the past." How mixed are our feelings. How fortunate we are that much of the past is long forgotten. How fortunate we are that the happy times remain embedded in our minds.

As I walk my dog along the sunny streets of Napa, I cannot help but smile as sunny days of my past come to mind. Days with my children. Days with my grandchildren. Now, days with my great-grandchildren. Days with no purpose. Sunny days of laughter and fun. I embrace the memories with an affection unlike any other.

My flights of memory do not cause me to yearn for a return to those earlier days. I relish the memory of all the joyous celebrations of love we shared over the years. And yet, nothing prepared me for the joys of my present life. Did I even know anyone enjoying life in their eighties?

Nostalgia might sweep over me at times. Listening to music of my past. Dance music from my high school years. Opera music that thrilled my heart with joy. Classical music heard on lonely days. A bird's song in the twilight of a dimming evening. The sound of the waves caressing the shore. All this and more give me cause to reflect and return for moments not forgotten.

Living the unexpected life of today is also something that causes me reflection. Nostalgia is swept away by the present. My heart is filled with appreciation. I now have time to reflect on the present. Every day is precious. Today's special moments are not only ours but those of all those we encounter. We have the power to amaze. All we say and do takes on a new meaning. We are the curious "old." Hopefully, we can leave a legacy of positive moments that will cause others to reflect on our lives when they reach our age. Nostalgia is for us and we can exist in it.

Floating Corpse

I awoke to find a dead body floating belly-down in the swimming pool. I had just poured my first cup of coffee for the day, and went into my backyard to check the bird feeders, when I saw the body. I live in a remote part of town where nothing seems to happen. Big shade trees make me feel private and secluded. What in the world could cause a stranger to come into my yard? My gardener came when he could, which wasn't often enough. How long had there been a body in my pool?

The pool hadn't been cleaned for a while. Dead leaves clouded the surface. At first, I wasn't even certain it was a body; it looked like a mess of old clothes someone had tossed into the pool. Whoever expects to see a floating corpse in their swimming pool?

One of the drawbacks of living alone is there is never a reason to scream because no one could hear you. So I did the next best thing—I called my friend, Paul. I knew he would be furious if he missed out on the excitement sure to follow. He lived on the next block and arrived before I finished explaining to the police over the phone that there was a dead person in my pool.

Paul didn't know who it was and neither did I. We were sure the police could not implicate us in any murder if we didn't recognize the corpse.

Still, it was my swimming pool. I had it fenced to keep the neighborhood kids out, knowing the laws are strict about fencing pools. I was always concerned about safety and had a locked gate on the fence and checked the lock regularly.

I had been sleeping very soundly the night before and did not hear anything. I told Paul to check the lock on the gate and he confirmed it was intact.

The police arrived right after Paul. Then came the fire truck and ambulance and all the neighbors. Good thing I had thrown on a robe. It all happened so fast, I didn't have time to get properly dressed. Summer nights don't call for much clothing in Southern California. I wasn't prepared to be examined by all and sundry as the possible murderer in my light pink baby doll pjs. I was glad I made a pot of coffee as the day dragged on. The police inspection took longer than I had anticipated. Thinking they may take me to police headquarters, I decided to dress. I wanted to look my most innocent just in case I was a suspect. I put on an old pair of jeans, a t-shirt, and grabbed my sweater.

Arriving at police headquarters after their inspection, I was handed a cup of coffee and told to wait for the arresting officer to complete his report. Seems identifying dead people takes more time than on TV. I glanced down at my shirt. It read *Ross Perot for President*. Seems like my grandma gave me this t-shirt as a joke. I quickly pulled my sweater over my chest and tried not to be seen—the unseen suspect.

Finally, the coroner arrived and announced the body was of a young man—early twenties, no tattoos, no scars, and no signs of violence. Still, drugs and alcohol could have played a part in his death. They had to wait for the results of a toxicology report. Meanwhile, I tried to think of any young men I may have encountered; the bagboy at the market, somebody's son, someone from church, someone from down the block. I drew a complete blank.

The arresting officer showed me a picture of the young man's face, thinking I should be able to identify him. A picture of a dead person is quite a bit different than one of a living person, yet he did seem familiar to me. I couldn't put my finger on why, though, but I knew I had seen him before. The officer watched me carefully and I took my time before I said no, I didn't know him. After fingerprinting, I was instructed to stay in the country to make it easy for them to find me.

Paul picked me up at the police station with all kinds of questions that I had no answers for. I told him that the young man looked like someone I knew but couldn't remember where I had seen him.

When finally my home was empty of all investigators, I felt like I had been whipped and needed to lay down. On my couch I let the TV drone on until the news came on with me the center of attention—Ross Perot t-shirt and all. That's when my telephone started ringing. At first, I answered it, but soon became tired of all the same questions that the police had asked. I didn't know who the man found dead in my pool was—or did I?

Since the phone wasn't going to quit ringing, I decided that I might as well clean the pool as it had been so neglected that the leaves were beginning to decompose. Besides that, I didn't want any reporters seeing it so dirty since they would probably want to take pictures of the place where the body was found.

It took hours to dip out the debris that had collected on the surface. Since the body had disturbed the surface, a lot of leaves had gone to the bottom of the pool. As I dipped and dumped the stuff, I swore that I would finally open up my purse and hire a dependable pool man to take care of it next time.

As I scooped out some of the leaves from the bottom of the pool, I saw a shiny glint in the dump pile. At first, I thought it was a button or coin. Parting the leaves and fingering through the debris that was left, I discovered a small metal key with a number on it. Could the key have opened the locked gate to the pool? No. It wasn't big enough. Was it a key to something in my house? No. I never locked anything, except for the pool. I wondered then if it had belonged to the dead man. I was sure it had something to do with the mystery of the floating corpse.

It was still bothering me that the body looked familiar. I tried to visualize where I might have seen him—maybe in a uniform of some kind. We see people all the time in our neighborhoods without really looking at them. The postman, an electrician, the ticket taker at the poll booth. It was driving me crazy.

Paul came over the next morning and I showed him the small key. He didn't know what it unlocked, either, but thought that maybe I should call the police and give it to them. He was right, of course. He offered to take the key to the police station to give me a little break. I was grateful for the offer and gave it to him.

I called the police station right after and had them send me a copy of the photo of the dead man's face. I also asked about the toxicology report. Sure enough, the alcohol level was way above what is considered the limit. Still no visible signs of violence. It appeared to be a drowning—perhaps the man had accidentally stumbled into my pool in a drunken stupor? But how did he get there in the first place? And why was the unfamiliar key at the bottom of my pool?

Once I had the picture, I showed it to Paul, wondering if he could recognize the dead man. Looking ashen as recognition set in, he said, "That is my sisters' boyfriend." That was where I had seen him! Paul's sister, Janet, had brought her boyfriend, Jerry, over to meet me. I had only seen him one time. We needed to contact the police with the name of the body—Jerry.

Then there was a knock at my door. My little dog, Snowy, barked and I suddenly became aware that he had not barked the night of the murder. It turned out to be another detective asking more questions. Since Paul was still there, we both sat down with the detective and we reviewed the facts. Paul explained the connection to him and showed the detective the key. The detective kept asking why Jerry was at my house, with me as puzzled as he was. We were getting nowhere. Since the previous day, I felt we were barraged by police questioning and getting farther and farther away from answers.

Just then, Danny, my almost "never available" pool boy stopped by. Of course, everyone wanted to know what was going on. I was curious why he stopped by all of a sudden but got rid of him as soon as I could and took Snowy for a walk. Paul seemed relieved that I didn't invite Danny in. I left Paul and the police officer talking about the last 49er football game and set out for a walk. As I walked past the fenced yard, I remembered that I had given Danny a key to the gate months ago when he last worked for me. Could he be involved in some way? It seemed that, today of all days, he decided to show up on my doorstep.

When he first started working to maintain my pool, he seemed like such a nice guy, and what a hunk! I hated to let him go. He was so undependable but I enjoyed his presence. As it turned out, all pool boys seem undependable. Oh well, he was fun to look at through the window as he cleaned the pool in his bathing trunks and then called me out for inspection. He cleaned all the pools in the neighborhood for a while. Then my neighbors began missing things and some thought Danny might have had something to do with it. I felt uncomfortable and let Danny go so the neighbors would stop their complaining.

Danny and Jerry were about the same age. Could there be a connection I was previously unaware of? I thought again about the key and suddenly remembered where I had seen a similar one. It had a number on it like the keys I had seen at the health club. I began to wonder if they were friends from the club. Did the key fit a locker there? Were they both in the yard the night Jerry died? That would explain how Jerry got into my yard. But why? Perhaps, my yard was the most secluded and convenient place to meet. The trees, shrubs, and fence would have concealed their meeting and Danny had a way to access it. No one would see them there. I headed home to alert the police that the key may have come from the health club.

Later that day, the police called to say they had opened the locker and found jewelry that appeared to be stolen and asked me to come down to the station to see if I could identify any of the items. On the way to the police station, Paul said he suspected that Danny and Jerry were in cahoots in stealing from the neighbors. He tried to ignore it as I had, but now had to tell his sister about the connection of the two and she confirmed that she, too, knew Danny and that he and Jerry were friends. Paul added he was suspicious that Danny killed Jerry to cover their crimes.

Janet was shocked but had to admit she knew Danny had a violent temper. That Jerry was involved came as a real blow. She had been curious as to Jerry's employment, because he always seemed vague when talking about work and where he got money, but never suspected him to be a thief. Now, Jerry was dead. The amount of stolen goods found in the locker made it evident that the robberies had been going on for some time.

Paul's sister was upset but later confessed that she suspected something crooked because Jerry always had money but didn't work much. She feared her boyfriend was in over his head with his relationship with Danny and knew he was dangerous. As it turned out that Jerry was indeed in over his head—drowned in the swimming pool.

New Old Friend

Go slowly. Choose wisely. My new motto.
Good rules for bridge and life.
Choice of partner is long lasting
Be it man or wife.

Playing the wrong card at bridge
Can cause the losing trick, making us wonder
At the carelessness of pick.
Discernment is the only way
To choose a friend or make the play.
We need our family and friends
To help us with our day to day.

Being settled in our peaceful home,
Time slips by and thoughts do roam.
Adventure once called us to explore,
To search for others and distant lands.
Now, we are bound by health and walls—
We are limited for fear of falls.

The joy we seek is revealed by others.
We no longer search for passionate lovers.
A kind smile, a tear, a hearty laugh
Brings memories of a distant past.

Could we but relive that time
That stays so embedded in our minds
And enjoy those memories with a friend
Those memories would find no end.

How much more of life there is to see
As we passionately await Eternity.
A true friend would surely enjoy
The vivid past my mind employs—

Tender moments as the heart rejoices
In songs of laughter, soft unspoken voices.
I recall a time gone by with a friend.
We relive the time in story and sigh.

Sharing old lives now and then
Brings back old feelings again and again.
"Be my friend," I yearn to extol
And I know somehow, very well,
That new friend and I can sit and recall
Our histories unknown and known
That remind our hearts we are not alone.

About the Author

When I reflect on my total life, I realize how truly fortunate I am to have had such a wonderful family. Starting at an early age with my grandmother, I always was surrounded with love. I was very special to my father. He would tell my mother "Don't disturb Brenda she's reading a book." At 13, he bought me my first horse in Galt. When we move to Colusa, he bought me another horse. I always had two horses so I could invite my friends to go riding. Looking back, I realized how spoiled I was. We were not a wealthy family, yet I always had horses and took flying lessons. I guess that's not the life of a regular teenage girl. Later life brought adventure and love in all its phases. I wouldn't change a minute. This book tells of some of the extraordinary moments I enjoyed growing up in the 1950s. My early life was not like any other time.